W9-BMQ-565

TAKE MY WIFE, PLEASE!

TAKE MY WIFE, PLEASE!

HENNY YOUNGMAN'S
Giant Book of Jokes

Illustrated by
Sheila Greenwald and Fred Hausman

A Citadel Press Book
Published by Carol Publishing Group

First Carol Publishing Group edition, 1998

Copyright © 1963, 1966, 1974 Henny Youngman
All rights reserved. No part of this book may be reproduced in any form, except by a newspaper or magazine reviewer who wishes to quote brief passages in connection with a review.

A Citadel Press Book
Published by Carol Publishing Group
Citadel Press is a registered trademark of Carol Communications, Inc.

Editorial, sales and distribution, rights and permissions inquiries should be addressed to Carol Publishing Group, 120 Enterprise Avenue, Secaucus, N.J. 07094

In Canada: Canadian Manda Group, One Atlantic Avenue, Suite 105, Toronto, Ontario M6K 3E7

Carol Publishing Group books may be purchased in bulk at special discounts for sales promotions, fund-raising, or educational purposes. Special editions can be created to specifications. For details, contact Special Sales Department, Carol Publishing Group, 120 Enterprise Avenue, Secaucus, N.J. 07094

Manufactured in the United States of America
ISBN 0-8065-2057-4

10 9 8 7 6 5 4 3 2 1

VOLUME ONE

How Do You Like Me So Far?

HENNY YOUNGMAN

Foreward by
MILTON BERLE

Drawings by Sheila Greenwald

To MY WIFE, whom I have abused constantly to our mutual profit.

To MY DAUGHTER MARILYN AND MY SON GARY, who had to spend many months alone while I was travelling.

To THE MEMORY OF MY FATHER

To MY MOTHER, AND MY BROTHER LESTER who travelled with me, and kept my hopes up at all times.

To MY IDOL, MILTON BERLE, who since the inception of my career as a comedian encouraged me and tried many of my jokes, and is still laughing at me.

The jokes in this book are my best. They are also the favorites of my friends in show business and in the newspaper field who have laughed and laughed when I told them. I especially owe the following a debt of gratitude for laughing the loudest:

Jackie Gleason
Bob Hope
Jan Murray
Harvey Stone
Joey Bishop
Don Tannen
Red Skelton
George Gobel
Dan Shapiro
Al Schwartz
Ed Sullivan
Walter Winchell
Leonard Lyons
Earl Wilson
Dorothy Kilgallen
Irv Kupcinet
Kate Smith
Sidney Piermont
Johnny Carson
Jack Paar
Joe Lefkowitz

Murray Kester
Joey Adams
Joe Gooter
Leo and Jean Fuld
Frank Farrell
Morey Amsterdam
Hy Goodbinder
Ted Collins
Archie Robbins
Milton Seiden
Walter Jacobs and
    family
Ida and Jack Mendes
Arthur I. Goldstein
Jimmy Kaplan
Estelle and Herman
    Davis
Hy Gardner
Jack Kalcheim
Frank Sinatra
Frankie Bradley

FOREWORD

Henny Youngman is one of the great comedians of our generation. This is not only my opinion. It's Henny's.

I've known Henny Youngman, man and joke file, for over thirty years. Unlike myself, Henny did not steal jokes from the top comedians of that era. Youngman stole from the unknowns, a word which later became synonymous with his career.

The greatest form of flattery is imitation, and one of Henny's unusual traits is that he is flattered by the fact that for many years he has been an imitation of a comedian.

Every top comedian has a special gimmick that makes him stand out above the others. Youngman's secret is in his delivery and his masterful ability to *segue* from one topic to another with such subtle-like blends as "I love California . . . Say didja hear about Mayor Wagner . . . My wife's in Miami now." Actually, Youngman hasn't got a routine, he has a master code. However, we in the business all envy Youngman's quick mind and his sharp retorts to hecklers. It was Youngman who put down a heckler many years ago with lines like "Oh, yeah?" and "Gee whiz."

I kid a lot about Henny, but actually he is one of

the fastest comedians around. He has to be, with *his* act. Henny Youngman is the only comedian who was asked to appear four times at the Court of St. James, and at each of these court appearances, he was convicted. Most comedians in the business love Henny Youngman, the same kind of love that Sybil Burton has for Liz Taylor.

I hope Henny Youngman has a lot of success.

Milton Berle

OPENING OF ALBUM

How do you like me so far?
I wasn't invited here, so I came here to see why
I wasn't invited.

I just finished filling out my income tax form. Who said you can't get wounded by a blank?

= = =

A Jewish woman had two chickens as pets. One chicken got sick, so she killed the other one to make chicken soup for the sick one.

= = =

A man can't find a lawyer, he picks up the Red Book, picks out a law firm—Schwartz, Schwartz, Schwartz & Schwartz. Calls up, he says, "Is Mr. Schwartz there?"
A guy says, "No, he's out playing golf."
He says, "All right, then let me talk to Mr. Schwartz."
"He's not with the firm any more, he's retired."
"Then let me talk to Mr. Schwartz."
"He's away in Detroit, won't be back for a month."
"Okay, then let me talk to Mr. Schwartz.
He says, "Speaking!"

= = =

I've got a brother-in-law who's a bookie. He's gotten thirty days so many times they're naming a month after him. He's working on a new invention that will kill television—color radio.

▭ ▭ ▭

A woman used to go to a doctor to see if she could have children. Now she goes to the landlord.

▭ ▭ ▭

The doctor opened the window wide. He said, "Stick your tongue out the window." I said, "What for?" He said, "I'm mad at my neighbors."

▭ ▭ ▭

My arm started to hurt me. I said, "Doctor, examine my arm." He looked at my arm, he brought out a medical book and studied it for fifteen minutes.
He said to me, "Have you ever had that pain before?"
I said, "Yes."
He said, "Well, you got it again."

▭ ▭ ▭

I have a very fine doctor. If you can't afford the operation, he touches up the X-rays. I went up to visit the doctor with my sore foot. He said, "I'll have you walking in an hour." He did. He stole my car.

A father was explaining ethics to his son who was about to go into business: "Supposing a woman comes in and orders $100 worth of material. You wrap it up and give it to her. She pays you with a $100 bill. As she goes out the door, you realize she has given you two $100 bills. Here's where the ethics come in. Should you or shouldn't you tell your partner?"

◻ ◻ ◻

John L. Lewis was down in Miami. He wore his seersucker eyebrows.

◻ ◻ ◻

I went down to Miami. They told me I'd get a lovely room for seven dollars a week. My room was in Savannah, Georgia.

◻ ◻ ◻

Every twenty minutes they change the rates. That's the only place you can go broke sleeping.

◻ ◻ ◻

Finally got a room and bath for thirty dollars a day. I didn't go to the beach once. I just stayed in my room and watched it.

◻ ◻ ◻

They gave me a lovely dressing room—a nail. That's the first time I ever had a dressing room where I had to tip the attendant. Everybody wants to help me carry my wallet.

To you people who are visiting: What makes you people so sure you turned off your gas back home?

□ □ □

In the next scene, we see a couple who have been married twenty years. He says to her, "Honey, let's go on a vacation." As he says this, he looks in the next room where he sees a little old lady knitting.

He says, "If you don't mind, let's go without your mother this time."

She says, "My mother. . . . I thought it was your mother all the time."

□ □ □

A lot of people are desperate today. A fellow walked up to me, he said, "You see a cop around here?" I said no. He said, "Stick 'em up!"

□ □ □

Another fellow walked up to me and said, "Stick 'em down."

I said, "You mean stick 'em up."

He said, "No wonder I haven't made any money."

□ □ □

I saw a drunk walk up to a parking meter and put in

18

a dime. The dial went to 60. He said, "How do you like that. I weigh an hour."

⊟ ⊟ ⊟

A drunk walked up to a parking meter and put in a dime. The dial went to 60. He said, "How about that. I lost 100 pounds."

⊟ ⊟ ⊟

Two drunks walking along Broadway in New York. One goes down into the subway by mistake. Comes up the other entrance and his friend is waiting for him.

The waiting drunk says, "Where were you?"

The other one says, "I was in some guy's basement. Has he got a set of trains!"

⊟ ⊟ ⊟

I saw a funny thing in Miami today. I saw a woman with a cloth coat.

⊟ ⊟ ⊟

There's a new perfume out which drives women crazy. It smells like money. It's called Filthy Lucre #5.

⊟ ⊟ ⊟

When I was a kid I had no watch. I used to tell time by my violin. I used to practice in the middle of the night and the neighbors would yell, "Fine time to practice violin, three o'clock in the morning!"

◫ ◫ ◫

What a voice I have. I'm the only one Mitch Miller begged not to sing along.

◫ ◫ ◫

I don't want to say I play fiddle bad. I'm the only one who played on "What's My Line?" and stumped the panel.

◫ ◫ ◫

Last night I ordered a whole meal in French and even the waiter was surprised. It was a Chinese restaurant.

◫ ◫ ◫

An art theatre: that's a place where the theatre is clean, the pictures are filthy.

◫ ◫ ◫

There's a new drink called Metrecal Scotch. You still

see the same things, but the elephants are skinnier.

□ □ □

They showed movies on the plane. The pilot wouldn't get on. He already saw the picture.

□ □ □

The plane was going up and down and sideways. A little old lady got nervous. She shouted, "Everybody on the plane pray."
So a man said, "I don't know how to pray."
She said, "Well, do something religious," so he started a bingo game.

□ □ □

I'm so near-sighted I can't even see my contact lenses.

□ □ □

A couple in Hollywood got divorced. Then they got remarried. The divorce didn't work out.

□ □ □

A rich guy in Dallas bought his kid a chemistry outfit —du Pont.

□ □ □

Did you hear about the rich kid from Dallas who walked up to Santa Claus and said, "Santa, what do you need?"

Want to drive somebody crazy? Send him a wire saying, "Ignore first wire."

⬒ ⬒ ⬒

Another way to drive a guy crazy: Send him a telegram and on top put "Page 2."

⬒ ⬒ ⬒

Mrs. Ponce de Leon to her husband Ponce: "You're going to Miami without me?"

⬒ ⬒ ⬒

You know what's embarrassing? When you look through a keyhole and you see another eye.

⬒ ⬒ ⬒

Want to have some fun? Walk into an antique shop and say, "What's new?"

⬒ ⬒ ⬒

In Hollywood they have community property. A couple gets divorced, she gets the Jaguar, he gets the little cap.

⬒ ⬒ ⬒

A stock broker calls up a client and says, "I think you should buy some Shapiro Uranium. It's 10¢ a share."

The client says, "Pick me up 20,000 shares at 10¢."

The next day the stock goes up to $1.00. The broker says, "You want to sell?"

The guy says, "No, get me 20,000 more shares."

The stock goes up to $3.00. "Buy me 20,000 more shares."

It goes up to $7.00. "Get me 20,000 more shares."

He says, "Sell me out at $7.00." The broker says, "To who?"

▭ ▭ ▭

I was in the lobby of the Sherman Hotel and I found a man's hand in my pocket. I said, "What do you want?"

He said, "I want a match."

I said, "Why don't you ask for it?"

He said, "I don't talk to strangers."

▭ ▭ ▭

My mother tells the joke about two little old ladies meeting. One says to the other, "What did you do to your hair? It looks awful—it looks like a wig."

She says. "It is a wig."

The other woman says, "You know, you could never tell."

▭ ▭ ▭

I love Christmas. I receive a lot of wonderful presents I can't wait to exchange.

⬚ ⬚ ⬚

A man went to Las Vegas with a $7,000 Cadillac and came home with a $75,000 bus.

⬚ ⬚ ⬚

In Las Vegas, a man walked up to his wife and said, "Give me the money I told you not to give me."

⬚ ⬚ ⬚

I've been married for thirty-four years and I'm still in love with the same woman. If my wife ever finds out, she'll kill me.

⬚ ⬚ ⬚

My wife has a nice even disposition. Miserable all the time.

⬚ ⬚ ⬚

Can she talk! She was in Miami, and when she got home, her tongue was sunburned.

⬚ ⬚ ⬚

She missed her nap today. She slept right through it.

□ □ □

Valentine's Day she gave me the usual gift. She ate my heart out!

□ □ □

She hasn't been feeling well lately. Something she agreed with is eating her.

□ □ □

I said to my mother-in-law, "My house is your house." Last week she sold it.

□ □ □

She needed a blood transfusion. We had to give up the idea. Couldn't find a tiger.

□ □ □

My wife went to the beauty shop and got a mud pack. For two days she looked nice. Then the mud fell off.

□ □ □

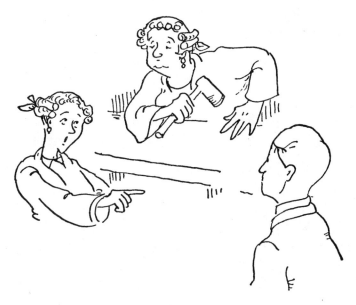

My wife should have been a lawyer. Every time we have an argument and she feels she's losing, she takes it to the higher court—her mother.

She puts that cold cream on at night an inch thick, and she puts those curlers in her hair, then she puts a fishing net over the whole thing.

She said, "Kiss me."

I said, "Take me to your leader."

▭ ▭ ▭

The way she looks in the morning! She ran after the garbage man and said, "Am I too late for the garbage?" He said, "No, jump in."

▭ ▭ ▭

Now she's on a diet. Coconuts and bananas. She hasn't lost any weight, but can she climb a tree!

▭ ▭ ▭

She's tried Metrecal, safflower oil—now she eats nothing but garlic and limburger cheese. Nobody can get near her, so from a distance she looks thin.

▭ ▭ ▭

I played a horse so slow the other day, the jockey kept a diary of the trip.

▭ ▭ ▭

I have a new album out in which I play my violin. It's
called "Music to Lose By."

□ □ □

Some people play a horse to win, some to place. I
should have bet this horse to live.

□ □ □

The jockey hit the horse, the horse turned around and
said, "What are you hitting me for? There's nobody behind us."

□ □ □

That's the first time I ever saw a horse start from a
kneeling position.

□ □ □

He was so late getting home, he tiptoed into the stable.

□ □ □

I don't mind when the horse is left at the post. I don't
mind when the horse comes up to me in the grandstand
and asks, "Which way did they go?" But when I see the
horse I bet on at the $2.00 window playing another horse
in the same race. . . .

I've got a brother-in-law who's a real character. Middle-aged man, still chases women, but forgets what for.

I wish he would learn a trade so we'd know what kind of work he was out of.

▭ ▭ ▭

One year he went in the breeding business. He tried to cross a rooster with a rooster. You know what he got? A very cross rooster.

▭ ▭ ▭

One time he crossed a parrot with a tiger. They don't know what it is, but when it talks, everybody listens.

▭ ▭ ▭

I just got him a job as a life guard in a car wash.

▭ ▭ ▭

I'll tell you how to beat the gambling in Las Vegas. As soon as you get off the airplane, walk right into the propeller.

▭ ▭ ▭

My mother came out there with me. Where do you think she was gambling? She was playing the stamp machine.

▭ ▭ ▭

Some man lost a lot of money in Las Vegas. He's fed up, he's disgusted, he's driving out of town. From out of the mountains he hears a voice saying, "Go back to Las Vegas, go back to Las Vegas."

He figures this is a good omen, he drives back to Las Vegas at eighty miles an hour. He gets back to Las Vegas, the voice says, "Go into the Sands Hotel to gamble this time."

So he goes into the Sands Hotel. The voice says, "Play roulette, put $2,000 on Number 8." He does that. Number 6 comes up. He loses. The voice says, "How about that!"

▭ ▭ ▭

This weather gets you nuts. One day it's cold, the next day it's nice—I don't know what to hock any more.

▭ ▭ ▭

You know, science is wonderful. It used to take you three years to get a tuxedo shiny. Now you buy it ready-made shiny.

▭ ▭ ▭

You know there's a new cloth you can wear in the rain. It gets wet, but you can wear it in the rain!

▭ ▭ ▭

I bought a suit that comes from London. It was brought here and sold to a wholesaler. The wholesaler sold it to a retailer and the retailer sold it to me. To think all those people are making a living out of something I haven't paid for.

▭ ▭ ▭

Once I asked Leo Durocher to get me seats for the World Series. He said, "Leave it to me." He got me seats. From where I sat, the game was just a rumor.

▭ ▭ ▭

I was up so high I was getting spirit messages.

▭ ▭ ▭

The usher took me half way up the stairs. He said, "You'll have to go the rest of the way yourself. From here on my nose starts to bleed!"

▭ ▭ ▭

I was the only one in my row without a harp.

▭ ▭ ▭

I said to the man next to me, "How do you like the game?" He said, "What game? I'm flying the mail to Pittsburgh."

＝ ＝ ＝

An actress in Hollywood got divorced, she took her four kids with her. There was an actor out there who got divorced, and he took his four kids with him. Then they met, they fell in love, they got married and had four kids of their own. One day she looked out the window, she said, "Darling, your kids and my kids are beating the heck out of *our* kids!"

＝ ＝ ＝

Want to have some real laughs? Go to your neighbor's house, go into the bathroom, lock the door, run a quarter of a tub of hot water and throw in twenty boxes of jello.

＝ ＝ ＝

A fellow walks into the Stage Delicatessen in New York and orders barley and bean soup. The Chinese waiter says, "Nemnisht," which means in Jewish, "Don't take that." The man was astounded. He walks over to Max, who owns the Stage Delicatessen and says, "Where did you get the Chinese waiter who speaks Jewish?" Max says, "Don't say anything. He's in the country four months—he thinks I'm teaching him English."

All you married men, want to drive your wives crazy? When you go home, don't talk in your sleep —just *grin*.

A fellow tries to cross the Mexican border on his bicycle. He's got two big bags on his shoulders. The guard says, "What's in the bags?"

He says, "Sand."

The guard says, "Get them off—we'll examine them."

The fellow takes the two bags off, they empty them out, they look through it, find nothing but sand. The guy puts the sand back in the bags, puts the bags back on his shoulders, the little fellow crosses the border on his bicycle.

Two weeks later, same thing. "What have you got there?"

"Sand."

"Get them off, we'll examine them."

They take them off, look through them and find nothing but sand. Put the sand back in the bags, back on the shoulders, he crosses the border on his bicycle.

Every two weeks for six months this goes on. Finally one week the fellow didn't show up and the guard meets him downtown.

He says, "Buddy, you had us crazy. We knew you were smuggling something. I won't say anything—what were you smuggling?"

The guy says, "Bicycles."

▭ ▭ ▭

A space man landed in front of Pumpernick's Delicatessen down in Miami Beach. The wheels on the airplane broke. He sees the bagels in the window. He walks in, he says, "Give me two wheels for my airplane."

The guy says, "These are bagels—you eat them."

He says, "Give me two wheels, I need them for my airplane."

The guy says, "These are bagels—you eat them—here, try one."

So the space man takes a bite of the bagel, he says, "You know, this would go good with lox."

▭ ▭ ▭

Some people ask, "What are your favorite jokes and how do you become a comedian?" Well, to become a comedian, you tell your friends a lot of jokes, you get them all together, you keep the good ones, before you know it you're a riot at a party. Somebody says, "You ought to go on the stage." Like an idiot, you believe them.

▭ ▭ ▭

Now to do this you must go to diction school. They teach you how to speak clearly. To do this they fill your mouth with marbles and you're supposed to talk clearly right through the marbles. Now every day you lose one marble. When you've lost all your marbles. . . .

▭ ▭ ▭

They've been making a lot of life stories in Hollywood. They made the life story of Jolson, they made the life story of Joe E. Lewis, they made the life story of Lillian

Roth. Why don't they make the story of my life? I might have lived.

◻ ◻ ◻

Here's my life story. I came from a very poor family. They couldn't afford to have children, so our neighbor had me.

◻ ◻ ◻

Things were rough when I was a baby. No talcum powder.

◻ ◻ ◻

Eleven kids in our family We were so poor we had to wear each other's clothes. It wasn't funny—I had ten sisters.

◻ ◻ ◻

My father was never home, he was always away drinking booze. He saw a sign saying "Drink Canada Dry." So he went up there.

◻ ◻ ◻

My father used to talk to me, he'd say, "Listen, Stupid,"—he always called me "Listen."

38

He didn't ask me to leave home, he took me down to the highway and pointed.

I met my first girl, her name was Sally. Was that a girl—was that a girl. That's what people kept asking.

⊟ ⊟ ⊟

Every girl has the right to be ugly, but she abused the privilege.

⊟ ⊟ ⊟

She had bags *over* her eyes.

⊟ ⊟ ⊟

She will never live to be as old as she looked.

⊟ ⊟ ⊟

Four drunks looked at her, they took the pledge.

⊟ ⊟ ⊟

It's the old story—she wanted furs, diamonds, sen-sen.

⊟ ⊟ ⊟

I never had a penny to my name, so I changed my name.

⊟ ⊟ ⊟

Uncle Sam called me. I flew my own plane for two years. Then the rubber band broke.

□ □ □

Sally, you were so bow-legged that when you sat around the house, you really sat around the house.

□ □ □

Your cute little nose—the way it turned up, then down, then sideways.

□ □ □

I can't forget the way your lovely hair grew halfway down your back. Too bad it didn't grow on your head.

□ □ □

Your left eye was so fascinating your right eye kept looking at it all the time.

□ □ □

I used to take you riding in my car, and you insisted I take the top down. It took me three hours. It wasn't a convertible.

□ □ □

A woman driver hit a guy and knocked him six feet in the air. Then she sued him for leaving the scene of the accident.

▱ ▱ ▱

Another lady hit a guy, she yelled, "Watch out!" He said, "What—are you coming back?"

▱ ▱ ▱

An Australian fag disgusted with the men in the U.S.A.: "I'm going back to my Sydney!"

▱ ▱ ▱

For a young man, it's wine, women and song. For me, it's Metrecal, the same old gal and "Sing Along With Mitch."

▱ ▱ ▱

I own a hundred and fifty books, but I have no book-case. Nobody will *lend* me a bookcase.

▱ ▱ ▱

Here's a recipe for a Thanksgiving turkey: Take a fifteen-pound turkey, pour one quart of Scotch over it and put it in the oven for half an hour. Take it out and pour one quart of gin over it, put it back in the oven for another half hour. Take it out and pour one quart of Burgundy wine over it, put it back in the oven for another half hour. Then you can take the turkey out of the oven and throw it out the window. But oh—what a gravy!

My mother-in-law, she's very modern. She uses L'Aimant Perfume, smells like the Coty girl, and looks like Mr. Clean.

They have a new thing nowadays called Nicotine Anonymous. It's for people who want to stop smoking. When you feel a craving for a cigarette, you simply call up another member and he comes over and you get drunk together.

It doesn't matter if you let money slip through your fingers, or even if you let love slip through your fingers; but if you let your fingers slip through your fingers, you're in trouble.

I went up to my tailor. I finally had enough money to have a suit made to order. The suit came out awful. All disheveled. I walked down the street. A fellow walked up to me and said, "Who is your tailor?"

I said, "Why?"

He said, "Anyone who can fit a deformed figure like yours is good enough for me."

When a woman puts on a dinner dress, it doesn't necessarily mean she's going to dinner. And when she dons a cocktail dress, it doesn't mean necessarily that she's going to a cocktail party. But when she puts on a wedding dress, you know she means business.

I'll never forget one day I was practicing the violin in front of a roaring fire and then my father walked in and he was furious. We didn't have a fireplace.

◻ ◻ ◻

Saw some swell ads in the paper the other day. "Young man, Democrat, would like to meet young lady, Republican. Object: third party!"

◻ ◻ ◻

I walked into a barber shop today and the guy nearly scared me to death. He was ordering supplies, and he ordered two bottles of hair tonic, one bottle of shaving lotion, and two dozen bottles of iodine!

◻ ◻ ◻

The cutest little girl was giving me a manicure. I said, "How's about a date later?"
She said, "I'm married."
I said, "So call up your husband and tell him you're going to visit a girl friend."
She said, "Tell him yourself—he's shaving you."

◻ ◻ ◻

You know, when I was a baby I cried an awful lot, but my mother said she wouldn't change me for a million.

46

My father said, "Maybe if you'd change him he'd stop crying."

□ □ □

One guy came home and said to his wife, "Someone showed me an amazing device that sews buttons right on clothes."

His wife said, "That's wonderful. What is it?"

And the guy said, "A needle and thread."

□ □ □

At the ball game today, one fellow started to bawl out the ump. Finally the ump was getting sore, so the fellow said, "I'm not really mad. This is just for the TV audience."

□ □ □

When I was a kid I had the cutest little button nose. But they couldn't feed me. It was buttoned to my lower lip.

□ □ □

My aunt said to her husband, "Max, last night I dreamed you bought me a fur coat." He husband said, "In your next dream, wear it in good health."

□ □ □

Calling all cops—calling all cops—be on the look-out
—they are passing a lot of counterfeit tens and twenties
—be careful when accepting bribes.

☐ ☐ ☐

You should have seen the shape on this girl. She looked
like a pair of pliers wearing a band-aid.

☐ ☐ ☐

I finally found out how they make ladies' bathing
suits. First they take a stitch of nylon. That's all!

☐ ☐ ☐

I wouldn't say her bathing suit was skimpy, but I saw
more cotton on top of an aspirin bottle.

☐ ☐ ☐

Somebody once asked me, "Henny, do you like bathing beauties?" I said, "I don't know, I never bathed
any."

☐ ☐ ☐

There's a new law that doesn't allow you to change
your clothes on the beach any more. But that doesn't

bother me. I change my clothes on the bus on the way down to the beach.

□ □ □

I fell asleep on the beach and burned my stomach. You should see my pot roast!

□ □ □

I like those chairs on the boardwalk in Atlantic City, the ones you sit in and a fellow pushes you. When I was playing there, I got in one and the fellow said, "Pardon me, but you look familiar to me."

I said, "My name's Henny Youngman, I'm appearing at the steel pier."

He said, "I saw your act!" So I got out and pushed him.

□ □ □

Have any of you folks seen me on television? Well, my wife must be right. She can't see me either.

□ □ □

One thing I like about the beach. There's nothing like getting up at 6:00 in the morning, putting on your bathing suit, jumping in the ocean, swimming out five or six miles, and then swimming back. There's nothing like it, so why do it?

□ □ □

A girl I knew came back from Miami so brown I gave her a practical birthday gift—saddle soap.

□ □ □

Doctors are worried about their public image these days. I don't wonder why. A few weeks ago a doctor friend of mine had trouble with his plumbing. The pipes in his bathroom began to leak. The leak became bigger and bigger. Even though it was 2:00 A.M., the doctor decided to phone his plumber. Naturally, the plumber got sore being awakened at that hour of the morning.

"For Pete's sake, Doc," he wailed, "this is some time to wake a guy."

"Well," the doctor answered testily, "you've never hesitated to call me in the middle of the night with a medical problem. Now it just happens I've got a plumbing emergency."

There was a moment's silence. Then the plumber spoke up. "Right you are, Doc," he agreed. "Tell me what's wrong."

The Doctor explained about the leak in the bathroom.

"Tell you what to do," the plumber offered. "Take two aspirins every four hours, drop them down the pipe. If the leak hasn't cleared up by morning, phone me at the office."

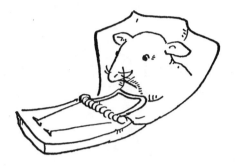

Fellow bought a mouse-trap for his cellar. When he went to set it, he found that he had forgotten to buy cheese, so he cut a piece of cheese from a magazine and placed this in the trap. Surprisingly enough this worked. When he went down the next morning, he found in the trap—a picture of a mouse.

I know a guy who used to be a test pilot in a suspender factory. But they let him go when they found out he was round-shouldered.

◻ ◻ ◻

Before that he worked in a winery, stepping on grapes. He got fired one day when they caught him sitting down on the job.

◻ ◻ ◻

My car is so worn out, every time I have to go down to the finance company to make a payment on it, I have to take a cab.

◻ ◻ ◻

I took my car down to see what I could get for it on a trade-in. One dealer took a look at it and offered me a ball-point pen.

◻ ◻ ◻

What a car! In order to go over ten miles an hour I have to remove the license plates. The car just won't pull that kind of a load.

◻ ◻ ◻

I took a look at my tires the other day. I've seen more rubber on the end of a pencil.

☐ ☐ ☐

Those aren't dents in my fenders, those are old-age wrinkles.

☐ ☐ ☐

Have you seen the new cars yet? They have a long pole sticking out in front with a boxing glove on the end of it. That's in case the car meets a woman driver, it fights back.

☐ ☐ ☐

I got a Volkswagen with four gears. The fourth gear is for going through Jewish neighborhoods.

☐ ☐ ☐

The two biggest features on the new cars are airbrakes and unbreakable windshields. You can speed up to one hundred miles an hour and stop on a dime. Then you press a special button and a putty knife scrapes you off the windshield.

☐ ☐ ☐

But the new cars are really something. One car
has a new safety device in case your wife is a back
seat driver. You press a button, a trap door opens
and she drops right out onto the highway.

I understand one company has a new car that tops them all. No clutch, no brake, no motor. There's only one trouble with it. They can't drive it out of the factory.

▭ ▭ ▭

And the color schemes on the new cars are terrific. One dealer offered me a choice—paint or wallpaper.

▭ ▭ ▭

This is National Gasoline Week. Be good citizens, get out on the highway and run out of gas.

▭ ▭ ▭

They've got a new batch of crazy songs nowadays. Have you heard "The Traffic Song"? U-U-U, you musn't make a U-U-U.

▭ ▭ ▭

I just solved the parking problem. I bought a parked car.

▭ ▭ ▭

Then there's a song called "Oh." It's a direct steal from a song I once wrote called "Ouch."

▭ ▭ ▭

More songs. "I'm Walking Behind You"—Please don't stop short! "I Saw Mommy Kissing Santa Claus" —in *November?* "I've Got the World on a String"— Hold tight everybody, I might let go.

▭ ▭ ▭

Then there's the song I sing to my wife every night— "P.S. I Love You." "P.S."—Poor Sadie.

▭ ▭ ▭

If anyone is thinking of sending me a Christmas gift this year, please don't bother. Just let me know where you live and I'll come and pick it up myself.

▭ ▭ ▭

I feel good today—I was up at the crack of six this morning. Took a brisk walk to the bathroom and was back in bed at 6:05.

▭ ▭ ▭

One fellow walked into the club and asked for change for twenty bucks, and they made him a partner.

▭ ▭ ▭

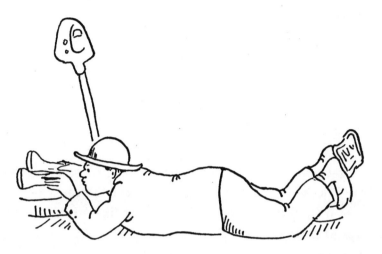

Things are rough. People are worried. I saw a man lying in the gutter, I walked up and said, "Are you sick? Can I help you?"

He said, "No, I found a parking space, I sent my wife out to buy a car."

A man called up and said, "What time does the show go on?"

"What time can you make it?" was the reply.

☐ ☐ ☐

One thing about this town, the Russians will never get here. No place to park.

☐ ☐ ☐

I get some fan mail from people. One letter said, "Dear Mr. Youngman: I think you are one of the most handsome men I have ever seen. I would like to meet you right after the show." Signed—"Bruce"!

☐ ☐ ☐

Another fan letter: "Dear Mr. Youngman: I am an ex-convict. I am a fan of yours. I am about to get out of jail shortly and am about to get married to a young lady who was also in jail. She'd like to know something about my family. Well, everybody knows my father used to take narcotics, my mother sold narcotics, I have a brother who's a used car dealer, and I have another brother who is now in jail for assault and battery. Do you think I should tell her about my brother who is a used car dealer?"

☐ ☐ ☐

My wife and I have our little fights. We had a fight last week. Nothing much—two police cars.

␣ ␣ ␣

She puts that mud on her face before going to bed at night. I say, "Goodnight, Swamp."

␣ ␣ ␣

My wife spends a fortune on cold creams and oils, puts them all over her body. I went to grab her, she slid out of bed.

␣ ␣ ␣

One thing I will say, she's very neat around the house. If I drop ashes on the floor, she's right there to pick them up. I throw my clothes down, she hangs them up immediately. I got up at three the other morning, went in the kitchen to get a glass of orange juice, I came back, I found the bed made.

␣ ␣ ␣

Walked into a store and said, "This is my wife's birthday. I'd like to buy her a beautiful fountain pen." The clerk winked at me and said, "A little surprise, huh?" I said, "Yes, she's expecting a Cadillac."

You've got to compromise when you're married. My wife wanted a fur coat, I wanted an automobile. We compromised. I bought her a fur coat, we keep it in the garage.

■ ■ ■

I bought her a mink outfit—a rifle and a trap.

■ ■ ■

She likes those little foreign cars. I bought her two— one for each foot.

■ ■ ■

If they get any smaller! I got hit by one, I had to go to the hospital and have it removed.

■ ■ ■

Three weeks ago she learned how to drive it. Last week she learned how to aim it.

■ ■ ■

I came home last night, by accident, and there's the car in the dining room.

I said to my wife, "How did you get the car in the dining room?"

She said, "It was easy. I made a left turn when I came out of the kitchen."

☐ ☐ ☐

We went for a ride, she went through a red light.
I said, "didn't you see that red light?"
She said, "So what? You see one red light, you've seen them all!"

☐ ☐ ☐

She put her hand out the window and signaled right, then left, then she erased it.
I said, "What kind of signal is that?"
She said, "I wanted to go right, then I wanted to go left, then I changed my mind—I rubbed it out."

☐ ☐ ☐

One day she drove up the side of a building and there was another woman driver coming down.

☐ ☐ ☐

Speaking of taxes—somebody somewhere must be speaking of taxes. Not me. Who's got any money left?

☐ ☐ ☐

Another guy asked me for a dime for a cup of coffee.

I said, "Coffee's only a nickel."

He said, "Won't you join me?"

A panhandler said to me, "Mister, I haven't tasted food for a week."

I said, "Don't worry, it still tastes the same."

⊟ ⊟ ⊟

You give these fellows money, what do they do? They gamble. I can lose my own money—and I do!

⊟ ⊟ ⊟

I love this town. I have a lovely hotel room and bath. A little inconvenient though. They're in two different buildings!

⊟ ⊟ ⊟

You can imagine how big my room is, though. I close the door and the door knob gets in bed with me. And I like it.

⊟ ⊟ ⊟

I put the key in the keyhole, I broke the window.

⊟ ⊟ ⊟

The room is so small, the mice are hunchbacked.

⊟ ⊟ ⊟

I called down to the desk. I said, "Is this room service?"

She said, "Yes."

I said, "Send up a room."

▭ ▭ ▭

Down in Miami I worked in a place called the Deauville Hotel. Very exclusive. Room service has an unlisted number.

▭ ▭ ▭

Some man made a lot of money in the market. He went down to Miami for the first time, fell in the pool. The life guard pulled him out, worked on him, saved his life. The man walks over to me and says, "What do you tip for a thing like that?"

▭ ▭ ▭

Those bell hops are tip-happy. They walk around with their hands outstretched. I was in my room, I ordered a deck of playing cards, and the man made fifty-two trips.

▭ ▭ ▭

A little kid on the plane was annoying me with the water pistol and the water in the face.

I said, "Kid, do me a favor."

He said, "What?"

I said, "Kid, go outside and play."

These kids are nuts today. I got a kid myself, ten years old. He's going to be eleven—if I let him!

He came home from school the other day, he said, "Mother, I had a fight with another kid—he called me a sissy."

She said, "What did you do?"

He said, "I hit him with my purse."

There's a new song from my latest picture which I play on the violin called "I Was a Teen-aged Chicken Plucker."

A drunk walked into court. The judge said, "My good man, you have been brought here for drinking."

The drunk said, "All right, Judge, let's get started."

A drunk walks into an elevator shaft, falls down ten flights. He's lying there bleeding. He says, "I said *up*!"

One fellow put a gun in my back. He said, "Stick 'em up."
I said, "Stick what up?"
He said, "Don't mix me up—this is my first job."

A man fell out of a tenth-story window. He's lying on the ground with a big crowd around him, a cop walks over and says, "What happened?"
The guy says, "I don't know, I just got here."

A little old lady walked up to a cop and said, "I was attacked—1 was attacked!"
He said, "When?"
She said, "Twenty years ago."
He said, "What are telling me now for?"
She said, "I like to talk about it once in a while."

A woman called up the Police Department and said, "I have a sex maniac in my apartment. Pick him up in the morning."

A little old lady goes into court, she wants a divorce. The judge says, "How old are you?"

"Sixty."

"How old is your husband?"

"Sixty."

"How long you been married?"

"Forty years."

"What do you want a divorce for?"

She says, "Aah, enough is enough."

▭ ▭ ▭

HECKLER JOKES

Please, Mister, I have only an hour to make a jackass out of myself. You have all night.

□ □ □

Some people bring happiness wherever they go. You bring happiness *whenever* you go.

□ □ □

If you had your life to live over again, don't do it.

□ □ □

If I'm not in bed by eleven at night, I go home.

□ □ □

An elderly man was visiting his doctor for a check-up. The doctor said, "Mr. Jones, you're sound as a dollar. You'll live to be eighty."

"But I am eighty," Mr. Jones says.

"See, what did I tell you?"

□ □ □

Know what I got for Father's Day? The bills from Mother's Day.

□ □ □

A woman went to her psychiatrist and said, "Doctor, I want to talk to you about my husband. He thinks he's a refrigerator."

"That's not so bad," said the doctor. "It's a rather harmless complex."

"Well, maybe," replied the lady, "but he sleeps with his mouth open and the light keeps me awake."

□ □ □

You know something about my wife? It takes her forty minutes to get her lipstick on. Why? Because she has a big mouth, that's why.

□ □ □

My son was annoying me the other morning, so I said, "Why don't you go out and play in the traffic?"

□ □ □

If you must drink while you're driving home, be sure the radio in the car is turned up loud. That way you won't hear the crash.

□ □ □

I always try to buy a little something for my wife, but I can never remember her measurements. However, I always find a salesgirl who is built like her. The other day I couldn't find a salesgirl built like my wife. One was taller. One was shorter. But a customer standing nearby was built exactly like my wife, so I said, "Excuse me, sir, what size are you?"

The other day I was offered a TV series. They want me to star in something called "The Rock and Roll Robin Hood." I dress in a black leather jacket. I ride around on a motorcycle. I carry a gun. The whole premise is that I steal from the rich . . . but I keep it.

▭ ▭ ▭

The other day I went down to the Internal Revenue Department. Thank heavens! I'm all paid up until 1947.

▭ ▭ ▭

Two kangaroos were talking to each other, and one said, "Gee, I hope it doesn't rain today. I just hate it when the children play inside."

▭ ▭ ▭

A rugged Texan, dripping with oil and Cadillacs, walked into an exclusive art gallery in New York with his nagging wife. In fifteen minutes flat the Texan bought six Picassos, three Renoirs, ten Cézannes, and thirty Utrillos. He then turned to his wife and with a sigh of relief said. "There, honey chile, that takes care of the Christmas cards. Now let's get started on the serious shopping."

▭ ▭ ▭

During a flight from New York to Los Angeles, a passenger who had been gazing out the window suddenly spied two engines on fire. He began shouting at the top of his lungs, "Two engines are on fire! Two engines are on fire!"

In a few short seconds panic and hysteria spread to the rest of the passengers. The pilot, equipped with a parachute, soon appeared in the passenger compartment. "Don't worry," he assured them, "I'm going for help."

I still love the oldie about the convict who was going to the electric chair and called his lawyer for some last advice. The barrister replied, "Don't sit down!"

■ ■ ■

There was a mix-up at the swank Fifth Avenue florist shop. Wrong cards were attached to two imposing floral wreaths. The one that went to a druggist moving to a new building read: "Deepest sympathy." The one intended for the funeral of a leading banker read: "Good luck in your new location."

■ ■ ■

Las Vegas is the only town in the country where you can have a wonderful time without enjoying yourself.

■ ■ ■

A man doesn't know what real happiness is until he's married. Then it's too late.

■ ■ ■

Show me a man with very little money, and I'll show you a bum.

■ ■ ■

I miss my wife's cooking—as often as I can.

□ □ □

One time I came home and my wife was crying because the dog had eaten a pie she made for me.
"Don't cry," I told her, "I'll buy you another dog."

□ □ □

I learned dancing from Arthur Murray. Later I found
it was more fun with a girl.

□ □ □

The other day a policeman stopped me going the
wrong way on a one-way street.
"Didn't you see the arrow?"
"Arrow? Honest, Officer, I didn't even see the
Indians."

□ □ □

The other day a friend of mine walked into a cigar
store and said to the salesgirl, "I'd like to buy a carton
of cigarettes."
The salesgirl smiled and said, "There are so many
brands. Which one would you like?"
My friend thought for a moment, then mentioned a

75

particular brand, whereupon the following conversation took place:

"Do you want the soft pack or the crush-proof box?"

"Soft pack."

"King size or regular?"

"King size."

"Filter tip or plain?"

"Filter tip."

"Menthol or mint?"

"Menthol."

"Cash or carry?"

"Forget it. I've broken the habit."

▭ ▭ ▭

Martha Raye kissed me. I lost my head completely.

▭ ▭ ▭

I don't have to do this for a living. I can always starve to death.

▭ ▭ ▭

My wife doesn't want to take weight off. She just wants to rearrange it.

▭ ▭ ▭

My best friend ran away with my wife, and let me tell you, I miss him.

□ □ □

My wife talks so much I get hoarse just listening to her.

□ □ □

The garage charged me twenty-five dollars for towing my car for a mile. I got my money's worth, though. I kept my brakes on.

□ □ □

I sent my income tax form in last week and didn't sign it. If they want me to guess how much I'll make, let them guess who sent it in.

□ □ □

Miami's so empty the life guards are saving each other.

□ □ □

What good is happiness? It can't buy you money.

□ □ □

I saved a girl from being attacked last night. I controlled myself.

□ □ □

There's a new safety device on cars now. If you want to turn right, press a button and a sign lights up that says, "I'm turning right." Press another button and it says, "I'm turning left." There's a special button for women drivers. It says, "I don't know what I'm going to do next."

□ □ □

My wife is learning how to drive. When the road turns when she does, it's a coincidence.

□ □ □

"All right, Charlie, I want you to walk inside the bank, anyone gets in your way, shoot him down. Grab all the money, come walking outside. I'll be sitting in the getaway car. And remember one thing. I'll be taking all the chances."

"You mean to tell me you want me to walk inside the bank, anyone gets in my way, shoot him down, grab all the money, come walking outside. You'll be sitting in the car waiting for me and you say you'll be taking all the chances? What chances are you taking?"

"I can't drive."

□ □ □

I never drink coffee during the day. It keeps me awake.

☐ ☐ ☐

I'm not overweight. I'm just six inches too short.

☐ ☐ ☐

I just found out why those guys ride bicycles up in the air on the tight wire. No traffic.

☐ ☐ ☐

"Young man, you have been brought in here for driving eighty miles an hour. What have you got to say for yourself?"

"Judge, I wasn't going eighty, I wasn't going sixty, I wasn't going forty or thirty or twenty or ten."

"Give him a ticket for backing into someone."

☐ ☐ ☐

I watched a new car roll off the assembly line. It's amazing. They start out with little pieces, then it rolls down the assembly line and thousands of men and a million dollars' worth of machinery put everything together. Finally a shiny new car emerges. Then a woman buys it and turns it into little pieces again.

☐ ☐ ☐

Two drunks were standing in front of the Washington monument. One of them started a fire at the base of it. The other said, "You'll never get it off the ground."

The darnedest things are happening in California. I just got back yesterday. I was in Beverly Hills and never saw so many foreign cars. Milton Berle was driving an American car. The people were yelling at him, "Yankee, go home."

□ □ □

When I was in Hollywood I watched them make the movie *Walk on the Wild Side*. It's about a guy who tries to get on the other side of the Hollywood Freeway.

□ □ □

Martha Raye's been married six times now. She's got a wash-and-wear bridal gown.

□ □ □

The trouble with my wife is that she goes for any new vogue that comes along. She saw a picture with Jacqueline Kennedy with the hemline above the knees, so she ran right out and had all her dresses shortened. The only difference is, my wife has knees like Peter Lawford's.

□ □ □

They're adding a new traffic light to the standard group of red, amber, and green. If you have an accident, this one squirts iodine.

□ □ □

A new model has the license plates on the bottom of the car. If a guy knocks you down, you can look up and see who hit you.

□ □ □

My wife changes her hair so many times she has sort of a convertible top.

□ □ □

They're remodeling St. Patrick's Cathedral. They're putting in drive-in confessionals. It's called "Toot and Tell."

□ □ □

He can't seem to find a job in his trade. He's a fog light operator in the steam room of a Turkish bath.

□ □ □

A guy is sending a wire to his partner. He tells the Western Union operator to say, "Don't come back. Business is bad, I just laid off twenty people, the bill collectors are after me." Then he says, "And don't read it back, operator. It's breaking my heart—I can't stand it."

□ □ □

Sam and Al had been partners for many years and they shared and shared alike in almost everything, including the affection of their pliable and rather hot-blooded secretary. One morning Sam came into Al's office extremely upset. "Al," he moaned, "something terrible has happened. Our secretary is going to have a baby. We are going to be a father." But Al, who was the calmer of the two, sat his partner down and pointed out that a great many worse things could have happened to them: Business could have fallen off, for instance. They agreed that the only thing to do was share and share alike, as they always had. They would see that their secretary got the very best in medical care, they decided, and after the child was born, he would want for nothing. A room of his own, fine clothes and the best of schooling; they would set up a trust fund after his birth to guarantee him a college education. The lucky youngster would have two fathers instead of just one. And before they knew it, the big day had arrived. The two of them paced back and forth in the hospital waiting room until Sam could stand it no longer. "I'm too nervous up here," he said. "I'm going to go down and sit in the car. As soon as something happens, you come down and tell me." Al agreed, and in less than an hour he was down on the street wearing a grave expression. It was obvious to Sam, even before his partner spoke, that something was wrong. "What's the matter?" Sam asked, starting to choke up. "Is it bad news?" His partner nodded. "We had twins," Al said, "and mine died."

▭ ▭ ▭

The place was so crowded you couldn't breathe in and out. You had to breathe up and down.

⊟ ⊟ ⊟

One new car is so modern you press a button and *it* presses a button.

⊟ ⊟ ⊟

My kid is a born doctor. That kid can't write anything anybody can read.

⊟ ⊟ ⊟

Some men sleep in pajama bottoms, some in pajama tops. I just sleep in the string.

⊟ ⊟ ⊟

Everybody's on strike nowadays. We saw a guy carrying a sign with nothing on it.

"Who are you picketing against?" I asked.

He says, "Nobody. I'm looking for a sponsor."

⊟ ⊟ ⊟

The income tax people are very nice. They're letting me keep my own mother.

▭ ▭ ▭

Time is so short on some of the TV programs. Just imagine yourself listening to a musical program with announcements and jokes at the same time.

▭ ▭ ▭

My brother-in-law has an allergy. He's allergic to work.

▭ ▭ ▭

A guy picks up a girl in a bar. She notices his cuff links and tie clasp have the insignia of a whip on them. He invites her for a ride in his Cadillac, and she notices on the door is the whip insignia, and even on the hub caps. On the cigarette lighter there's the whip insignia. They go to his apartment and there's the whip motif again on the chairs, on the bar, everywhere. He says, "I'm going to change into something more comfortable," and disappears into the bedroom. She notices a picture on the wall of a half-naked man with a whip in his hand, beating a woman. He comes back into the room wearing a smoking jacket with a whip insignia on it and says to her, "Now I'm going to make love to you."
She says, "Thank God."

We got a new foreign car with the motor in the back. Pulled up in front of the Sherman Hotel and the bell-boy opened up the back of the car. Before I knew it, the motor was up in the room.

□ □ □

The meanest thing you can do to a woman is to lock her in a room with a thousand hats and no mirror.

□ □ □

Christine Jorgenson's mother is doing a book—*My Son, the Daughter.*

□ □ □

A fellow is standing in a bar and another guy walks up to him and says, "Are you Joe Smith?"

The fellow says, "Yes, I'm Joe Smith."

He says, "Were you in Chicago a few weeks ago?"

The fellow says, "Just a minute," and takes a little notebook out of his pocket and riffles through the pages, goes down the line, and says, "Yeah, I was in Chicago a few weeks ago."

"Did you stay at the Sherman House?"

The guy looks through his little notebook again and says, "Yes, I stayed at the Sherman House."

"Were you in Room 213?"

The fellow scans the pages of his notebook again and says, "Yes, I was in Room 213."

The guy says, "Did you know a Mrs. Wentworth who stayed in Room 214?"

The guy looks in his book again and says, "Yes, I knew a Mrs. Wentworth who stayed in 214."

The guy says, "Tell me, did you have an affair with Mrs. Wentworth?"

The fellow scans his notebook again and says, "Yes, I had an affair with Mrs. Wentworth."

The guy says, "Well, I'm Mr. Wentworth, and I don't like it."

Again the fellow looks into his notebook and says, "You know, you're right. I didn't like it either."

⊟ ⊟ ⊟

One beauty shop makes your hair curly for only 49¢. They stick your finger in the light socket.

⊟ ⊟ ⊟

The traffic was so heavy people were driving bumper to bumper. I pushed in my cigarette lighter and the woman in the car in front of me said, "Ouch!"

⊟ ⊟ ⊟

President Kennedy met my wife. He declared my home a disaster area.

⊟ ⊟ ⊟

To give you an idea how difficult my wife can be, she bought me two ties for my birthday. To please her I wore one. She hollered, "What's the matter, don't you like the other one?"

▭　▭　▭

Saw something funny in the paper today. "Father of 14 Shot—Mistaken for Rabbit."

▭　▭　▭

He said, "I love you terribly." She said, "You certainly do."

▭　▭　▭

I know a guy that was so active that five years after he died, his self-winding watch was still running.

▭　▭　▭

The automobile of tomorrow will be faster than sound. You'll be in the hospital before you start the motor.

▭　▭　▭

Now that I've learned to make the most of life, most of it is gone.

▭　▭　▭

My wife keeps imitating Teddy Roosevelt. She runs from store to store yelling, "Charge!"

Paying alimony is like having the TV set on after you've fallen asleep.

░ ░ ░

My wife used to be a guitar player. She got rid of the guitar and now just picks on me.

░ ░ ░

A fellow walked up to me today and asked for a nickel for a cup of coffee. I gave it to him, and then followed him to the restaurant.

░ ░ ░

The first part of our marriage was very happy. But then on the way back from the ceremony. . . .

░ ░ ░

A guy buys all kinds of scuba diving equipment—$2,000 worth. He goes 150 feet down in the water, sees all the strange fish and scenery, and says to himself, "This is really worth $2,000—I'm really enjoying it." He goes down another 50 feet, sees more beautiful fish and scenery, and all of a sudden coming toward him is a fellow in just plain swimming trunks. He takes out his underwater pad and pencil and writes a note to the guy in the trunks saying, "I just spent $2,000 on all this scuba equipment and here you are all the way down in just a pair of swimming trunks. What's the idea?"

He hands the pad and pencil to the man, who writes back, "You idiot—I'm drowning."

▭ ▭ ▭

Things are rough with me. Just got a letter from my bank. It says, "This is the last time we will spend 5¢ to let you know you have 4¢.

▭ ▭ ▭

Americans are getting stronger. Twenty years ago it took two people to carry ten dollars' worth of groceries. Today a five-year-old does it.

▭ ▭ ▭

The other day I was driving under the influence of my wife. She talks and talks and talks. She gets two thousand words to the gallon.

▭ ▭ ▭

I gave my wife a car. She loves it so she's taking it to England. She wants to see what it's like to drive on the left side of the street—legally.

▭ ▭ ▭

When I was a kid, I practiced. The neighbors threw stones through the window. Imagine being that anxious to hear me play! I was flattered.

   ▭ ▭ ▭

I've got a sixteen-year-old son who is 6′3″ until he gets a haircut. Then he's 5′8″.

   ▭ ▭ ▭

Drunk to traffic cop: "But nobody in the car was driving, Officer. We were all in the back seat."

   ▭ ▭ ▭

I have a great house. It's just twenty minutes from the city—by phone.

   ▭ ▭ ▭

Statistics show that every four seconds a woman gives birth to a baby. Our problem is to find this woman and stop her.

   ▭ ▭ ▭

Have you tried vodka and carrot juice? You get drunk just as fast, but your eyesight gets better.

   ▭ ▭ ▭

A guy goes to a psychiatrist and says, "I keep dreaming that Liz Taylor wants to take me in her arms and I keep pushing her away."

The doctor says, "My advice to you is, break your arms off."

◻ ◻ ◻

A guy comes up in divorce court about alimony payments. The judge says, "The Court shall grant this woman twenty-five dollars a week."

The guy says, "That's very nice of you, Judge. I'll pitch in a few dollars myself."

◻ ◻ ◻

Three scientists were given six months to live and told they could have anything they wanted. The first scientist was a Frenchman. He wanted a beautiful villa on the Riviera and a gorgeous woman. The second doctor was an Englishman. He wanted to have tea with the Queen. The third doctor was a Jewish doctor. He wanted the opinion of another doctor.

◻ ◻ ◻

Business was so bad the other night the orchestra was playing "Tea for One."

◻ ◻ ◻

It was so bad the cigarette girl was selling loose cigarettes.

Whisky certainly improves with age. The older my brother-in-law gets, the better he likes it.

⊟　⊟　⊟

I live so far out of town in the suburbs, the mailman mails me my letters.

⊟　⊟　⊟

Did you ever see one of those Italian movies, "Bread, Love and Pizza," or "Bread, Love and Mozarella"? What are all the lovers over there, bakers?

⊟　⊟　⊟

They're making a new picture with Brigitte Bardot. She's fully dressed and the camera men are naked.

⊟　⊟　⊟

Lately my wife's been falling in love with television heroes. When she gets a sore throat, she refuses to go to a doctor. She sits in front of the TV set with her mouth open, showing her tonsils to Ben Casey.

⊟　⊟　⊟

Do you know what it means to come home at night to a woman who'll give you a little love, a little affection, a little tenderness? It means you're in the wrong house, that's what it means.

□ □ □

He's the kind of a guy who drinks Brazilian coffee out of an English cup while devouring French pastry while sitting on his Danish furniture after coming home in his German car from seeing an Italian movie, then blows his top, picks up his Japanese-made ball-point and writes to his Congressman, demanding that they stop the flow of gold out of this country.

□ □ □

It's easy to grin when your ship comes in
And life is a happy lot,
But the guy worthwhile is the guy who can smile
When his shirt creeps up in a knot.

□ □ □

A man seventy-five years old is reading in his hotel room when he hears a knock on the door and a beautiful girl says, "I'm sorry, I must be in the wrong room."
He says, "You got the right room, but you're forty years too late."

□ □ □

All you people in from out of town—what makes you so sure you turned off your TV sets back home?

□ □ □

Two guys who work in the garment industry are hunting game in Africa. They hear the growl of an animal behind them.
One says, "What kind of an animal is that?"
The other says "What am I—a furrier?"

□ □ □

A guy in the garment industry has a son who asks him, "Daddy, what kind of a flower is that?"
He says, "What am I, a milliner?"

□ □ □

Two guys in the industry were having lunch together.
One guy says, "Oye."
The other one says, "You're telling me!"

□ □ □

I don't know what to get my wife any more. First she wanted a mink, I got her a mink. Then she wanted a silver fox, I got her a silver fox. It was ridiculous. The house was full of animals.

□ □ □

A guy comes home and finds his wife relaxing in bed. All looks well till he notices a cigar in the ash tray. He becomes furious and yells, "Where did that cigar come from?"

A voice from under the bed says, "Havana!"

◻ ◻ ◻

One day in school young Johnny wrote on the blackboard, "Johnny is a passionate devil." The teacher reprimanded him for this act, and made him stay after school for one hour.

When he finally left the school that evening, all his friends crowded around him, eager to hear what punishment he had received. "What did she do to you?" asked one little tyke.

"I ain't saying nothing," Johnny replied, "except that it pays to advertise."

◻ ◻ ◻

A middle-aged friend of ours says he can't understand all the excitement over the movie version of *Lolita*. "I didn't see anything in it that could be considered even vaguely sensational," he told us, "and neither did my twelve-year-old wife."

◻ ◻ ◻

The convertible glided silently to a stop on a lonely country road.

"Out of gas," he said, with a sly smile.

"Yes, I thought you might be," said his date, as she opened her purse and pulled out a small hip flask.

"Say, you *are* a swinger," he said. "What do you have in there—Scotch or Bourbon?"

"Gasoline," she replied.

"My wife is always asking for money," complained a friend of ours. "Last week she wanted $200. The day before yesterday she asked me for $125. This morning she wanted $150."

"That's crazy," we said. "What does she do with it all?"

"I don't know," said our friend, "I never give her any."

□ □ □

The unabashed dictionary defines adolescence as the age between puberty and adultery.

□ □ □

Noah Webster's wife, returning from a long trip, discovered the lexicographer "in flagrante delicto" with a pretty chambermaid. "Mr. Webster!" she gasped, "I am surprised!"

"No, my dear," said Webster with a reproving smile. "You are shocked; I am surprised."

□ □ □

Hoping to avoid the embarrassing attentions that most hotels bestow on newlyweds, the honeymooners carefully removed the rice from their hair, took the "Just Married" sign off their car, and even scuffed their luggage to give it that traveled look. Then, without betraying a trace of their eagerness, they ambled casually into Miami

Beach's Fontainebleau Hotel and up to the front desk, where the groom said in a loud, booming voice, "We'd like a double bed with a room."

⊟ ⊟ ⊟

The unabashed dictionary defines incest as sibling revelry or a sport the whole family can enjoy.

⊟ ⊟ ⊟

Many a girl succeeds in keeping the wolf from her door these days by inviting him in.

⊟ ⊟ ⊟

In her own eyes, Peggy was the most popular girl in the world. "You know," she said, with characteristic modesty, "A lot of men are going to be miserable when I marry."

"Really?" said her date, stifling a yawn. "How many are you going to marry?"

⊟ ⊟ ⊟

We just got the word about the legal secretary who told her amorous boy friend, "Stop and/or I'll slap your face."

⊟ ⊟ ⊟

Sugar daddy: A man who can afford to raise Cain.

□ □ □

A gravedigger, thoroughly absorbed in his work, dug a pit so deep one afternoon that he couldn't climb out when he had finished. Come nightfall and evening's chill, his predicament became more uncomfortable. He shouted for help and at last attracted the attention of a drunk staggering by.

"Get me out of here," the digger pleaded. "I'm cold!"

The inebriated one peered into the open grave and finally spotted the shivering digger in the darkness.

"Well, no wonder you're cold, buddy," said the drunk, kicking some of the loose sod into the hole. "You haven't got any dirt on you."

□ □ □

We know a girl who thinks she's a robot just because she was made by a scientist.

□ □ □

A man is old when his dreams about girls are re-runs.

□ □ □

Alimony: Bounty on the Mutiny.

□ □ □

The psychiatrist leaned back and placed the tips of his fingers together while he soothed the deeply troubled man who stood before him. "Calm yourself, my good fellow," he gently urged. "I have helped a great many others with fixations far more serious than yours. Now let me see if I understand the problem correctly. You indicate that in moments of great emotional stress, you believe that you are a dog. A fox terrier, is that not so?"

"Yes, sir," mumbled the patient. "A small fox terrier with black and brown spots. Oh, please tell me you can help me, doctor. If this keeps up much longer, I don't know what I'll do."

The doctor gestured toward his couch. "Now, now," he soothed, "the first thing to do is lie down here and we'll see if we can't get to the root of your delusion."

"Oh, I couldn't do that, Doctor," said the patient. "I'm not allowed up on the furniture."

□ □ □

A manager brings a dog into a night club to work. The dog is a brilliant piano player—plays Bach, Beethoven, everything. He's sitting there playing and all of a sudden a big bushy-haired dog comes in and pulls him off the stool. The owner of the club says to the dog's manager, "What happened?"

He says, "Ah, they want him to be a doctor."

□ □ □

Nieman Marcus in Dallas is very good to their customers. A woman broke her leg, they had it gift wrapped.

I want to send my brother-in-law a gift for Christmas. What do you give a guy who's had everybody?

⬜ ⬜ ⬜

Taxes are still going up. Somebody has to pay for Caroline's piano lessons.

⬜ ⬜ ⬜

It was so crowded at Macy's, I rested my elbow on the counter and somebody sold it for $1.98.

⬜ ⬜ ⬜

I will never forget my school days. I was teacher's pet. She couldn't afford a dog.

⬜ ⬜ ⬜

There's nothing wrong with my wife that a miracle won't cure.

⬜ ⬜ ⬜

My wife eats so fast she makes sparks come out of her knife and fork.

⬜ ⬜ ⬜

I went to a very swanky party the other day. They didn't serve napkins, the waiters walked around with roller towels.

A bunch of ten guys had a very poor friend, a real hard-luck guy they wanted to help out. They decided to have a raffle and let him win, so they made all the tickets number 4 except his. They put all the tickets in a hat and let him draw. He sticks his hand in the hat and pulls out 6⅞.

      ▭   ▭   ▭

A friend of mine was complaining that the new house he rented had grass growing through the living room floor.

I asked, "How much rent are you paying?"

He said, "Forty dollars a month."

I said, "What do you expect for forty dollars a month —broccoli?"

      ▭   ▭   ▭

I used to be a fighter. They used to call me Canvas-back Youngman.

      ▭   ▭   ▭

I used to go into the ring vertical and come out horizontal.

      ▭   ▭   ▭

I had so much resin on my back that whenever I passed Carnegie Hall the fiddles used to stand at attention.

☐ ☐ ☐

I was the first guy to fight a four-way cold tablet six ways.

☐ ☐ ☐

I did pretty good at the beginning, I won my first ten fights, then I ran into trouble. They made me fight a man.

☐ ☐ ☐

What a fight! When the bell rang, I came out of my corner and threw six straight punches in a row. Then the other guy came out of his corner.

☐ ☐ ☐

First he threw a right cross, then he threw a left cross. Then came the Red Cross.

☐ ☐ ☐

He came up to about my chin. The trouble was he came up too often.

□ □ □

My best punch was a rabbit punch, but they would never let me fight rabbits.

□ □ □

In the fifth round I had my opponent worried. He thought he killed me. But in the sixth round I had him covered with blood—mine!

□ □ □

My favorite sport now is baseball. I went to the game today. It seems everybody went to the game today. The subways were so crowded even the men were standing.

□ □ □

But I'm always a gentleman in the subway. Whenever I see an empty seat I point it out to a lady, then I race her for it.

□ □ □

A terrible thing happened to me on the subway. The paper I was reading got off at Ninety-sixth Street.

You meet the craziest people on the subway. One guy sitting next to me kept saying, "Call me a doctor—call me a doctor."

I asked, "What's the matter, are you sick?"

He said, "No, I just graduated from medical school."

⌧ ⌧ ⌧

Another guy kept running around the train yelling, "I'm George Washington—I'm George Washington." The conductor yelled, "Valley Forge," and the guy got off.

⌧ ⌧ ⌧

I just bought a little Italian car. It's called a Mafia. There's a hood under the hood.

⌧ ⌧ ⌧

Jack the Ripper was never killed. I think he's doing my shirts.

⌧ ⌧ ⌧

Income tax: That's the government's version of instant poverty.

⌧ ⌧ ⌧

A little boy never said a word for six years. One day his parents served him cocoa. From out of left field the kid says, "This cocoa's no good."

His parents went around raving. They said to him, "Why did you wait so long to talk?" He said, "Up till now everything's been okay."

＝ ＝ ＝

We got a new garbage disposal—my brother-in-law. He'll eat anything.

＝ ＝ ＝

There's a new kind of push-button car. In case you get stuck in heavy traffic, you push a button, you get out and take a cab.

＝ ＝ ＝

Want to get a bootblack crazy? Next time you go in for a shine, wear one black shoe and one brown shoe.

＝ ＝ ＝

A guy walks into psychiatrist's office and says, "Doc, I'm going crazy. I keep imagining I'm a zebra. Every time I look at myself in the mirror my entire body seems covered with black stripes."

The doctor says, "Now calm down, go home and take these pills, get a good night's sleep and I'm sure the black stripes will disappear." The guy goes home, takes the pills, and comes back two days later. He says, "Doc, I feel great. Got anything for the *white* stripes?"

▭ ▭ ▭

Have you noticed the album covers lately? Beautiful pictures of gorgeous, well-built girls. You open it up and what've you got? A flat record!

▭ ▭ ▭

Just found a labor-saving device—a rich old lady.

▭ ▭ ▭

Whistler's mother was doing a handstand. Her son asked, "What's the matter, Ma, you off your rocker?"

▭ ▭ ▭

There's a new kind of Russian roulette. You get six cobras in a room and you play a flute. One of them is deaf.

▭ ▭ ▭

My dad was the town drunk. A lot of times that's not so bad—but New York City?

▭ ▭ ▭

Did you hear about the near-sighted snake who fell in love with a piece of rope?

You see some of the craziest things in restaurants. I saw a guy put ten spoons of sugar into his coffee and then start to drink it. I said, "How come you don't stir it?"

He answered "I don't like it sweet!"

□ □ □

When it comes to gambling, I only gamble for laughs. In fact, last week I laughed away my car.

□ □ □

There's a new medical show. It's called Perry Casey. It's about a lawyer who owns his own ambulance.

□ □ □

They had a fire in a hotel in Miami Beach. A woman shouted, "Help—fire—Cha-Cha-Cha!"

□ □ □

Say, what do you send to a sick florist?

□ □ □

ADVICE JOKES

Question: My child has a nail-biting habit. How can I stop him from biting his nails all the time?

Answer: That's easy, lady. Just have his teeth yanked out.

Question: Two men are in love with me, Murray and George. Who will be the lucky one?

Answer: Murray will marry you. George will be the lucky one.

Question: I've been married for five years and my husband still keeps his old address book. Is that fair?

Answer: Of course that's fair. When you buy a new car you always carry a spare, don't you?

Question: I like to read a book and am constantly annoyed by my small son sliding down the banister. How can I stop him from sliding down the banister?

Answer: Put some barbed wire on the banister. That won't stop him, but it will certainly slow him down.

Question: I came home late one night and my wife began hitting me with a baseball bat. When she got tired, her six brothers and her father all took turns hitting me with the bat. Is that legal?

Answer: It's perfectly legal for a woman to hit her husband with a baseball bat, but she is not allowed to bring in so many pinch hitters.

My wife is the sweetest, most tolerant, most beautiful woman in the world. This is a paid political announcement.

▭ ▭ ▭

PSYCHIATRIST JOKES

I went to see a psychiatrist. He said, "Tell me everything." I did, and now he's doing my act.

▭ ▭ ▭

A mother took her little boy to a psychiatrist and asked, "Can a boy ten years old marry a beautiful star like Liz Taylor?"

The psychiatrist said, "Of course not, it's impossible."

The mother said to the kid, "See, what did I tell you. Now go and get a divorce."

▭ ▭ ▭

Another woman took a little kid to a psychiatrist and said, "Doctor, my boy keeps eating grapes all the time."

The psychiatrist asked, "What's wrong with that?"

"Off the wallpaper!"

My wife is probably the world's worst cook. She has a certain knack of preparing food that's inedible. She cooks from a recipe book called *Condemned by Duncan Hines*.

▭ ▭ ▭

You should taste some of the dishes she prepares. Did you ever eat baked water?—French fried mustard?—pickled fortune cookies?

▭ ▭ ▭

Last year she made me a birthday cake with the candles on the inside! Lit!

▭ ▭ ▭

But I'm just kidding. I love my wife. In fact, I just bought her a present—a new set of stationery, a ball-point pen, and a pound of butter. Every time I go out of town she writes me a greasy love letter.

▭ ▭ ▭

In my house I don't need any long-playing records, not with *my* wife around.

▭ ▭ ▭

The good Lord played me a dirty trick. Instead of a tongue he gave her a permanent needle.

□ □ □

Nothing confuses a man more than driving behind a woman who does everything right.

□ □ □

Take my wife—please!

□ □ □

My mother-in-law is not with us. She's in the Congo teaching them to fight dirty.

□ □ □

How do you like this new tuxedo—$300. You don't believe it? I'll show you the summons.

□ □ □

When you're down and out, lift up your head and shout, "Help!"

□ □ □

I want to send my brother-in-law a gift. How do you wrap up a saloon?

❑ ❑ ❑

A woman is taking a shower. All of a sudden her doorbell rings. She yells, "Who's there?"

He says, "Blind man."

Well, she's a charitable lady. She runs out of the shower naked and opens the door.

He says, "Where should I put these blinds, lady?"

❑ ❑ ❑

I want to tell you, I have lived. You should have been here Tuesday night. Somebody should have been here. I don't want to say business was bad, but the doorman got locked up for loitering.

❑ ❑ ❑

Liz Taylor! Take away her long black hair and what have you got? The sexiest bald-headed woman in the world!

❑ ❑ ❑

I forgot your first *and* your last name.

❑ ❑ ❑

My wife always complains about something. She always complains about the housework. So I went out and bought her an electric iron, an electric dishwasher, and an electric dryer. She complained—too many gadgets. She had no place to sit down. What do I do to make her happy? I went out and bought her an electric chair.

▭ ▭ ▭

Every place is so jammed nowadays. To get to the other side of the street you have to be born there.

▭ ▭ ▭

Hear about the gypsy who doesn't read the tea leaves? She reads the lemon.

▭ ▭ ▭

I just heard from Bill Bailey. He's not coming home.

▭ ▭ ▭

I just got my TV set insured. If it breaks down they send me a pair of binoculars so I can watch my neighbor's set.

▭ ▭ ▭

But I respect women drivers. I always give them half of the road, when I can figure out which half they want.

◩ ◩ ◩

There's a new device on cars to protect you against teen-age drivers. When you see a teen-ager coming, you press a button. The car folds into the glove compartment till the kid goes by.

◩ ◩ ◩

Would you believe it, I used to play at Carnegie Hall —till the cops chased me away.

◩ ◩ ◩

I feel great. I paid my income tax this month. If anybody has a piece of crayon, please color me broke.

◩ ◩ ◩

At the rate the Kennedys are going, the Republicans won't have a chance. I understand all the Kennedy kids held a meeting up at Hyannis Port last week and decided to apply for statehood.

◩ ◩ ◩

Speaking of taxes, everybody is worried about entertainment expenses. The government wants you to keep a diary. I went out with some people the other night. I marked everything down—fifty dollars for food, thirty dollars for champagne, ten dollars for tips. The government disallowed it. They found out I was a guest.

□ □ □

I know of one guy who was called in by the tax department and showed up with 400 little black diaries all filled with expenses.

They asked, "What business are you in?"

"I sell little black diaries."

□ □ □

The whole thing is ridiculous. You take somebody to lunch, you can't write it off unless you talk business. I took a blonde to lunch the other day. I started to talk business, she slapped me right in the face.

□ □ □

Just imagine a hot phone between Russia and the United States. If someone accidentally pushes the wrong button, the operator will cut in and say, "Sorry, you have just reached a disconnected nation."

□ □ □

Of course the Republicans are worried about the expense. They sent a note to Jack Kennedy saying: "If you have to use the hot phone, do it after 9:00 o'clock at night. The rates are cheaper."

▭ ▭ ▭

I hate to take my wife to the movies. She lives the part of every picture she sees. I took her to see *Days of Wine and Roses*. She went home and forced herself to get drunk. I took her to see *The Music Man*. For six months she took trombone lessons. Next week I'm taking her to see a picture she won't have any trouble with— *The Ugly American*.

▭ ▭ ▭

Everybody is trying to cooperate with President Kennedy's physical fitness program. I know a wealthy guy in Texas who did not have the time to go on a fifty-mile hike, so he sent his butler.

▭ ▭ ▭

My wife is crazy about furs and she wanted something different. So she went to a furrier who does his own breeding. He crossed a mink with a gorilla. She got a beautiful coat, only the sleeves are too long.

▭ ▭ ▭

I've been getting a lot of fan mail lately asking me how I can play the violin so badly. I'll let you all in on a secret—the answer is wet resin.

☐ ☐ ☐

Do you know that Jack Benny and I took lessons from the same teacher? *Nero.*

☐ ☐ ☐

In conclusion I leave you with the words of a famous pro football player, who said: "It's not the way you play the game, it's the way you *bet* that counts."

☐ ☐ ☐

Before I go, I have a message for all you parents. Is your teen-age son or daughter out for the evening? If so, take advantage of the opportunity. Pack your furniture, call a moving van, and don't leave a forwarding address.

VOLUME TWO

Henny Youngman
400 Traveling Salesmen's Jokes

Drawings by Fred Hausman

400 Traveling Salesmen's Jokes

There's a parallel between a Martini and a woman's breasts: One is not enough; three are too many.

With a bushel of apples, you can have a hell of a time with the doctor's wife.

The two Madison Avenue types met on the suburban train platform.

"Hi, Charley," greeted the one, "How's your wife?"

"Compared to what?" responded the other dryly.

HOLLYWOOD: The city where they put beautiful frames in pictures.

11

A Texas oil man went in to see his dentist, and when asked which tooth was bothering him, replied, "Oh, just drill anywhere, doc. I feel lucky today."

Carter had been back from his honeymoon only a week when a friend asked him how he liked married life.

"Why, it's wonderful," was his enthusiastic reply. "It's almost like being in love."

College: A fountain of knowledge where all go to drink.

Sipping her second Alexander, the green-eyed secretary said to her girlfriend, "You've been dating Harold since you were both kids and the relationship doesn't seem to be going anywhere. Hasn't he any ambitions?"

"Oh, yes," smiled her sexy companion, "ever since he's been knee-high."

After an engagement of several years, George and Gloria were finally married. When they returned from their honeymoon, a bright-eyed friend asked Gloria how she enjoyed being married.

Absent-mindedly, the bride replied, "To tell the truth, I can't see a bit of difference."

12

The bountifully endowed young doll was in an embarrassing situation, for her arms were filled with packages and she was wearing a dress too tight to allow her to step up into the bus. A crowd pressed from behind, and so she reached back, unobserved she hoped, and attempted to gain some additional freedom by pulling down the zipper at the back of her dress. It didn't seem to help, so she reached again for the zipper and additional freedom, but again it was no use.

Then, from out of the crowd behind her, a young man picked her up and deposited her gently inside the bus.

"What right have you to pick me up like that?" she gasped. "Why I don't even know you."

"Well, miss," the man said, "after you pulled my zipper down the second time, I began to feel as though we were pretty good friends."

While making love to his wife, Carl discovered he couldn't concentrate. Though they were married only a few years, he reflected unhappily, their lovemaking had become infrequent and essentially joyless.

Then, suddenly alarmed, he cried, "What happened? Did I hurt you?"

"No," said his surprised wife. "Why do you ask?"

"No reason, really," he replied with a sigh. "It was just that for one moment there I thought you moved."

OLD MAID: A girl of 24—where she should be about 36.

Sunday was to be the day of Joe's wedding, and he and his father were enjoying a nightcap together. Lifting his glass in a toast to his father, Joe asked: "Any advice before I take the big step, dad?"

"Yes," the father said. "Two things. First: insist on having one night out a week with the boys. Second: don't waste it on the boys."

The girl who stoops to conquer usually wears a low-cut dress.

There was a drunk sitting in a bar, crying like a baby. A guy walked up and asked what was wrong.

"I did a terrible thing tonight," sniffled the drunk. "I sold my wife to a guy for a bottle of Scotch."

"That is terrible," said the other guy. "And now that she's gone you wish you had her back."

"That's right," said the drunk, still sniffling.

"You're sorry you sold her because you realize too late that you love her."

"No, no," said the drunk. "I wish I had her back because I'm thirsty again."

"But, Robert," she gasped, "why did you park here when there are so many nicer spots farther down the road?"

He stopped what he was doing just long enough to mutter, "Because I believe in love at first site."

BACHELOR: A rolling stone who gathers no boss.

With due respect to old Charlie Darwin, although man has learned enough through evolution to walk in an upright posture, his eyes still swing from limb to limb.

NUDISM: Exposure with composure.

A pair of good friends, Frenchmen both, were strolling down the Champs-Elysées one day when they spied two women approaching.

"Sacrebleu, Pierre!" cried one. "Here comes my wife and my mistress walking toward us arm in arm."

"Mon Dieu, Henri!" cried out the second. "I was about to say the very same thing."

A hitchhiker was picked up by a rich Texan driving a big, expensive convertible. As they drove along the open highway, doing well over fifty, the hitchhiker noticed a pair of very thick glasses on the seat between them.

"Are those glasses yours?" the hitchhiker asked nervously, noticing that the Texan was staring intently at the road before him.

"Yep. Wouldn't go no place without them. Can't hardly see my hand in front of my face when I don't have them on. But don't worry," he said, noticing the hitchhiker's uneasiness, "this here windshield is ground to my prescription."

FOOTBALL GAME: A contest where a spectator takes four quarters to finish a fifth.

A cute young thing was consulting a psychiatrist. Among other questions, the doctor asked, "Are you troubled at all by indecent thoughts?"

"Why, no," she replied with a twinkle in her eye. "To tell you the truth, Doctor, I rather enjoy them."

A beautiful girl was talking to her psychiatrist about her problem.

"It's liquor, doctor. Whenever I have a few drinks I have a compulsion to make love to whomever I happen to be with."

"I see," said the doctor. "Well, suppose I just mix us up a couple of cocktails, then you and I sit down nice and relaxed and discuss this compulsive neurosis of yours."

FALSIES: Extra padded attractions.

Many a man has been slapped because his hand was quicker than the aye.

Homer and his pretty wife were about to check out of the hotel when Homer expostulated over the amount of the bill. The hotel manager told him that was the normal rate for a double room with bath and TV.

Homer said they didn't use the TV.

"I'm sorry, sir," said the manager. "It was there for you to use if you'd wanted it."

"O.K.," said Homer, "but in that case I'm going to charge you for making love to my beautiful wife."

The manager denied it, and Homer said, "That's O.K. She was there for you to use if you wanted to."

The manager was so flustered he reduced Homer's bill and Homer decided to try it again the next time they went on a trip.

"Sir, that's our normal rate," said the young clerk.

"But we didn't use the TV."

"I'm sorry, but it was there for you to use if you wanted to."

"In that case I'll have to charge you for making love to my beautiful wife."

To Homer's chagrin the young man stammered, "O.K., O.K., I'll pay you. But keep your voice down, will you? I'm new at this hotel and you're apt to get me fired."

Ye Middle English edition of the Unabashed Diction-ary defines chastity belt as an antitrust suit, and the unchivalrous knight as the one who files it.

First prize at a recent costume ball went to a young woman wearing a maternity jacket over her dress, to-gether with the sign: "I Should Have Danced All Night."

Beauregard discovered his wife in the arms of her lover. Mad with rage, he shot her dead. The southern jury brought in a verdict of justifiable homicide.

Just as Beauregard was about to leave the courtroom a free man, the judge stopped him and asked, "Why did you shoot your wife instead of her lover?"

"Suh," he replied, "I decided it was better to shoot a woman once than a different man each week."

Year in and year out, although other colors may make a momentary bid on the fashion scene, the most popu-lar among women remains long green.

Assault: What every woman lies to be taken with a grain of.

A friend of ours has just told us about a remarkable ploy that's used by an aging and wealthy man-about-town. He dates only the most beautiful girls, and confides to each of them that he suffers from a heart condition (not true). Then, he takes them home to his magnificent estate, where they are properly dazzled by the quantity and quality of his possessions. He hints at the vast extent of his fortune.

Then comes the clincher: he tells each wide-eyed, open-mouthed girl that by the terms of his will all his money and possessions go to whomever is with him at the time of his death.

Then, so he claims, the girl usually does her level best to kill him with kindness.

GIGOLO: A fee-male.

A castaway was washed ashore after many days on the open sea. The island on which he landed was populated by savage cannibals who tied him, dazed and exhausted, to a thick stake. They then proceeded to cut his arms with their spears and drink his blood. This continued for several days until he could no longer stand it.

He called the cannibal king and said, "You can kill me, but this torture with the spears has got to stop. Dammit, I'm tired of being stuck for the drinks."

Latest rags-to-riches story—Texas style—concerns a young man from Dallas who inherited five million dollars, and proceeded to run it into a small fortune.

ECSTASY: Something that happens between the Scotch and soda and the bacon and eggs.

"Daughter," said the suspicious father, "that young man who's been walking you through the park strikes me as being exceedingly unpolished."

"Well," she answered coyly, "he *is* a little rough around the hedges."

What some young ladies refer to as a diary might be more aptly described as a whodunit.

FALSIES: Absentease.

Having received a return from a bachelor executive who claimed a dependent son, an income tax inspector sent the form back with a note saying, "This must be a stenographic error."

Back came the report, with the added notation, "You're telling me."

A number of showgirls were entertaining troops at a remote army camp. They had been at it all afternoon and were tired and very hungry. At the close of their performance, the major asked, "Would you girls like to mess with the enlisted men or the officers this evening?"

"It really doesn't matter," spoke up a shapely blonde. "But we've just got to have something to eat first."

Wilbur had always been a busy, tense man and his doctor informed him he would have to quit working and rest for a year. His wife Mildred lovingly agreed to support them for a year, but she was not a bright girl, and the only profession she was qualified for was the world's oldest. At the end of her first day out, she arrived home a sorry sight, in a state of near-exhaustion.

"How much did you earn, dear?"

"Thirty-six dollars and a quarter."

"That isn't very much for 12 hours' work. Who gave you a quarter?"

"Why, silly," she said. "All of them, of course."

While down south on a visit, the young Yankee made a date with a local lovely. When he called for her, she was clad in a low-cut, tight-fitting gown. He remarked, "That's certainly a beautiful dress."

"Sho 'nough?" she asked sweetly.

"It sure does," he replied.

Sheila and George were spending the first night of their honeymoon in a quaint medieval town in France. Sheila suggested coyly that they make love every time the old night watchman rang his hourly bell. George smiled in delight at this prospect, but four rings later he pretended he had to go out for cigarettes and staggered off to the watchman's tower.

"Listen, old man," he wheezed, "do me a favor and for the rest of the night ring that bell at two hour intervals instead of hourly, Here, I'll give you some money."

"I would be happy to oblige," said the watchman, "but I cannot. A beautiful young lady has already bribed me to ring the bell every half hour."

A rape case was being tried in a Hollywood court. The victim, a movie starlet, was on the stand. "Now young lady, please tell the court what happened. First, can you identify the man?"

"That's the one," she said, pointing.

"And please tell the court when this occurred."

"Yes sir. As I remember, it was last June, July, August and September."

When the traveling salesman's car broke down, he stopped at a farmhouse, and was invited to sleep with the farmer's daughter. They went to bed, and he made a pass. She said, "Stop that or I'll call my father." He tried again. She said, "Stop that or I'll call my father." But she moved closer. Finally, he succeeded. Shortly after, she tugged on his pajama sleeve, and said, "Could we do that again?" He obliged. A little later, she woke him up and asked if they could do it again. He obliged. The third time she woke him up and asked if they could do it again, he said, "Stop that or I'll call your father."

A new housekeeper accused of helping herself to her master's liquor said, "I'll have you know, sir, that I come from honest English parents."

He said, "I'm not concerned with your English parents. What's worrying me is your Scotch extraction."

The Unabashed Dictionary defines offspring of a prostitute as brothel sprouts.

The Unabashed Dictionary (Las Vegas edition) defines naturalist as a fellow who throws sevens.

"How about joining me for a cozy weekend in a quiet suburban hotel?" he whispered in her ear.

She said, "I'm afraid that my awareness of your proclivities in the esoteric aspects of sexual behavior precludes such an erotic confrontation."

"I don't get it," he said.

"Exactly," she smiled.

A gourmet friend of ours advises that when preparing a dish for bedtime, champagne makes the best tenderizer.

FALSIE SALESMAN: A Fuller bust man.

"I take the next turn, don't I?" asked the driver of the car.

A muffled reply came from the back seat: "Like hell you do."

Deciding to investigate rumors of immoral amusements among college students, a young professor arranged to have himself invited to a weekend party.

After the party had been going for several hours without a single incident, the much-relieved prof said goodnight, and went up to bed.

Suddenly, his door opened, and a shapely coed in a flimsy nightgown appeared.

"Did you want me?" he asked in surprise.

"Not especially," she said. "I just drew you."

HARP: A nude Steinway.

The maître d'hôtel at the Ritz was interviewing waiters for a big society banquet. The only applicants he could find were inexperienced or had had experience at hash houses. He could do nothing but hire them.

During the banquet one of the waiters noticed that a young debutante's bosom had fallen out of her gown and was in her soup. Quick as a flash he jumped forward, seized it, dried it with a towel and put it back in her gown.

The maître de seized him and denounced him as a clumsy oaf. He said, "When an incident such as that occurs at the Ritz, one uses a warmed serving spoon."

LESBIAN: A mannish depressive with delusions of gender.

"What are you reading?" asked the prison librarian.

"Nothing much," replied the prisoner. "Just the usual escape literature."

A man is incomplete until he's married. Then he's really finished.

The Italian government is installing a clock in the leaning tower of Pisa. Reason? What good is it if you have the inclination and you don't have the time?

Some of the best bedtime stories can be found in motel registers.

"Say," said the operator in his usual confidential tone, "there's a lot of good stuff at this party. If I find a chick who's ready, would you mind if I used your extra bedroom for a quick tryst?"

"Not at all, but what about your wife?"

"Oh, I'll only be gone a few minutes. She'll never miss me."

"No, I'm sure she won't miss you," said the host, "but fifteen minutes ago *she* borrowed the extra bedroom."

CENSOR: A person who sticks his No's in other people's business.

A good golfer has to break 80, but a good chorus girl only has to bust 36.

The other evening in a bar, a rather shy friend of ours spotted a remarkably stacked young lady drinking alone a few stools away. He moved over and sat next to her, but he was too embarrassed to talk. So, instead, when he ordered his next drink, he ordered one for her and paid for them both. She nodded her thanks, but still they did not speak.

This went on for four rounds. Finally, emboldened by the liquor, he said, "Do you ever go to bed with men?"

"I never have before," she said, smiling, "but I believe you talked me into it, you clever, silver-tongued devil, you."

George knew just what he wanted in a woman.

"The girl I marry," he used to say, "will be an economist in the kitchen, an aristocrat in the living room, and a harlot in bed."

Now he's married, and his wife has all the required traits—but not in the same order. She's an aristocrat in the kitchen, a harlot in the living room, and an economist in bed.

"Do you know what virgins eat for breakfast?" he asked.

"No, what?" she replied coyly.

"Hmmmm," he said, "just as I thought."

Strip poker is the one game in which the more you lose, the more you have to show for it.

The head doctor at the hospital was making his rounds, and he paused before a group of newborn babies. "What's the matter with this little fellow? He seems awfully puny and underweight."

The nurse said, "He's one of those artificial insemination babies, and I'm afraid he's been coming along rather slowly."

"Confirms a pet theory of mine," said the doctor. "Spare the rod and spoil the child."

Simple George was no great catch, so when he met a beautiful girl who seemed to be wildly in love with him, he immediately proposed.

"Darling," she said, "don't you realize that I'm a nymphomaniac?"

He said, "I don't care if you steal, as long as you're faithful to me."

One of our favorite drinks is a French eggnog—two egg yolks, two teaspoons of sugar, and four jiggers of cognac in a tall, warm lass.

"Wasn't it lovely out there on the lake?" he asked.

"It's lovely anyplace," she said.

BACHELOR APARTMENT: A wildlife sanctuary.

Returning from his vacation, Roger asked for two weeks more in which to get married.

"But you just had two weeks off," said the boss. "Why didn't you get married then?"

"What, and ruin my vacation?"

After numerous complaints from the neighbors, Harry sadly agreed to have a veterinarian render his cat fit to guard a sultan's harem.

"I'll bet," said one neighbor, "that that ex-Tom of yours just lies on the hearth now and gets fat."

"No, he still goes out at night. But now he goes along as a consultant."

The blonde appeared at her door in a strapless evening gown that defied gravity.

"Terrific," said her date. "I don't see what holds that dress up."

"Play your cards right and you will," she murmured.

33

Lily couldn't imagine why she was so popular.
"Is it my lovely hair?" she asked a friend.
"No."
"Is it my cute figure?"
"No."
"My personality?"
"No."
"Then I give up."
"That's it!"

Since the sweet young thing was warned by her mother not to talk to strange men, she only speaks to those who act familiar.

Two models were conversing chicly on a street corner when a third went riding by in a brand-new compact car.
"I understand," said one, "that she did it for a Lark."

HANGOVER: The wrath of grapes.

If, as the scientists say, sex is such a driving force, why is so much of it nowadays found parked?

To the astonishment of his friends, Martin, a gay blade, announced his intentions to marry. Speculations ran high as to what his conduct would be after the nuptuals, but Martin put an end to all doubt when he toasted the bridesmaids at the reception.

"Girls," he said, "I want to wish you all the best of luck, and to extend the hope that each of you will, in the near future, take the place of the bride."

The tensions of life were threatening to get a strangle hold on Bill, and after he'd finished a good dinner, he relaxed mindlessly in a soft chair next to the stereo, with a stiff drink in his hand. His wife knew nothing of his nervous state, and she climbed onto his lap with the thought of trying to wheedle a fur coat out of him, and snuggled and murmured and fondled.

"Good heavens, Ethel," he exploded, "get off. I get enough of this at the office."

Rules are the means of a girl's assessing which man she likes well enough to break them for.

The dean of women was introducing a visiting politician to the students.

"I couldn't begin to tell you all of the senator's accomplishments," she said, "but as an indication, you'll be interested to know that he has a nine-inch *Who's Who.*"

EXECUTIVE SUITE: A sugar daddy.

Spencer, the well-tailored man-about-town, walking ruefully out of court after getting stung by the decision in a paternity suit, was overheard to remark, "When I make a beaut, it's a mistake."

We've heard of a new low in community standing: a man whose credit rating is so bad his money isn't accepted.

Some girls are music lovers. Others can love without it.

DRIVE-IN MOVIES: Wall-to-wall car-petting.

A man will often take a girl to some retreat in order to make advances.

LEGAL SECRETARY: Any girl over eighteen.

Sue lay sprawled in sweet exhaustion on the bed, wearing a red ribbon in her bright blond hair. Beside her, Mark lit two cigarettes and passed one to her. For a long moment smoke and silence filled the air. Then she said, "My mother always told me to be good. Was I?"

Many a girl owes the fact that she's a prominent figure to a prominent figure.

The real estate agent couldn't remember when he'd rented an apartment to a more desirable tenant.

"Well," he said, "that's that. I wish you much happiness in your new apartment, and here are the two keys that come with it."

She accepted the keys and favored him with a dazzling smile.

"And here is a month's rent in advance, honey." And she handed him back one of the keys.

Women are to blame for most of the lying men do. They insist on asking questions.

The party was a smoothly swinging scene, with all the lights turned low, and Clark spied a female form alone in a corner. He crept up behind her and clasped her in a passionate embrace."

"How dare you!"

"Pardon me. I thought you were my sister."

"You chowderhead—I *am* your sister!"

A girl can be poor on history, but great on dates.

Too often, when you tell a secret to a girl, it goes in one ear and in another.

Grace and Martha were from a very prim and proper eastern finishing school, and they were spending their vacations together in New York. They met a bohemian artist and at one of his exhibitions Grace noticed that a canvas of a provocative nude bore a striking resemblance to her girlfriend.

"Martha," she gasped, "that painting looks exactly like you. Don't tell me you've been posing in the nude."

"Certainly not," Martha stammered, blushing furiously. "He must have painted it from memory."

Mike had just moved into a new apartment, and decided to get acquainted with his neighbors across the hall. He knocked on the door and was greeted by a young lady considerably more than passing fair, and considerably less than fully clad.

"Hi," he said. "I'm your new sugar across the hall. Can I borrow a cup of neighbor?"

The biggest difference between men and boys is the cost of their toys.

Many girls like the quiet things in life—like the folding of a hundred-dollar bill.

Some women can take a man to the cleaners as soon as they spot him.

PROTEIN: A call girl too young to vote.

Tom went to his friend's house and asked to be put up for the night because he had a fight with his wife.

"What happened?" the friend asked.

"When I got home tonight I was really beat, tired as hell. So when she asked me for fifty dollars for a new

40

dress, I guess I must have been half asleep or something, because I said, 'All right, but let's finish the dictation first.' "

We know a girl who is truly electric. In fact, everything she owns is charged.

The best years of a woman's life are usually counted in man-hours.

LATE DATE IN PARIS: Keeping a girl up until the oui hours of the morning.

Many a girl is looking for an older man with a strong will—made out to her.

The forgetful professor left his hotel room and discovered he had left his umbrella behind. He went back to get it and found that the room had been rented already. Through the door he heard sounds.
"Whose little baby are you?"
"Your little baby."
"And whose little hands are these?"
"Your little hands."
"And whose little feet are these—and whose little knees—and whose little—"

41

"When you get to an umbrella," said the professor through the door, "it's mine."

The history of women's fashions is a movement from skirts that barely cover the instep to skirts that barely cover the step-ins.

It was the young Englishman's first visit to the States and, in his innocence, he sought lodging in the city's red light district. When asked how his accommodations were, he replied, "Well, the room was very pretentious, you know, but gad, what maid service!"

Two hipsters were crossing the Atlantic by steamship. They were out on deck, looking at the ocean, and one said, "Man, look at all that water out there!"
"Yeah, man," the second, farther-out cat replied. "And just think, like that's only the top of it."

We know a college professor who claims that you'll always have a student body where you find a faculty for making love.

One prostitute said to another, "Would you please lend me ten dollars until I get back on my back?"

The board members of the catsup company were wowed by their new billboard. It showed a smart husband type seated before a delectable steak in a smart restaurant. A pretty young waitress was handing him a bottle of catsup. They decided the title, "What Does She Know About Your Husband That You Don't?" was too suggestive, so they changed it to, "He Gets It Downtown, Why Not Give It to Him at Home?"

Three young women were attending a class in logic, and the professor stated he was going to test their ability at situation reasoning.

"Let us assume," he said," he said, "that you are aboard a small craft alone in the Pacific, and you spot a vessel approaching you with several thousand sex-starved sailors on board. What would you do in this situation to avoid any problem?"

"I would attempt to turn my craft in the opposite direction," said the redhead.

"I would pass them, trusting my knife to keep me safe," said the brunette.

"Frankly," murmured the blonde, "I understand the situation but I fail to see the problem."

REPEAL: A stripteaser's encore.

Some girls ask the boss for advances on next week's salary. Others ask for salary on next week's advances.

There's a new organization called "Athletics Anonymous." When you get the urge to play golf, baseball, or anything else involving physical activity, they send someone over to drink with you until the urge passes.

WINDOW DRESSER: A girl who doesn't pull down the shades.

A friend of ours who is a nut on classic automobiles bought a car that runs entirely on electricity. He paid $10,000 for it—$5,000 for the car and $5,000 for the extension cord.

Bobby's mother had been away for a few weeks and was questioning her small son about events during her absence.

"Well, one night we had a thunderstorm, and I was scared, so daddy and me slept together."

"Bobby," said the boy's pretty young French nursemaid, "You mean 'daddy and I.'"

"No," said Bobby. "That was last Thursday. I'm talking about Monday night."

Some girls get a lot out of a dress, and leave it out.

The guy who first said "you can't take it with you" had probably never met an old maid.

STALEMATE: Last season's girlfriend.

Carol was furious when she came home and found her husband in bed with a lady midget.

"You promised you'd never cheat on me again."

"Well, as you can see, I'm tapering off."

Some girls think it's fun to fight against being kissed, while others prefer to just take it lying down.

Two friends were confiding to each other about their sex lives.

"You know," said one, "I never had any relations with my wife at all before we were married. Did you?"

"I don't know. What was her maiden name?"

47

The courtroom was pregnant with anxious silence as the judge solemnly considered his verdict in the paternity suit before him. Suddenly, he reached into the folds of his robes, drew out a cigar, and ceremoniously handed it to the defendant.

"Congratulations. You have just become a father."

Give some girls an inch and they've got a new bathing suit.

The man who can read women like a book usually likes to read in bed.

Flustered and flushed, Carol sat in the witness chair. The beautiful but empty-headed blonde had gotten herself named as corespondent in a divorce case.

"So, Miss Jones, you admit that you went to a hotel with this man."

"Yes, but I couldn't help it—he deceived me. He told the clerk at the reception desk that I was his wife."

Whoever it was who first called women the fair sex didn't know much about justice.

FALSIES: Hidden persuaders.

HAPPY MARRIED COUPLE: A husband out with another man's wife.

MAIDEN AUNT: A girl who never had sense enough to say uncle.

PROPOSAL: A proposition that lost its nerve.

SHOTGUN WEDDING: A case of wife or death.

VICIOUS CIRCLE: A wedding ring.

The popular girl is the one who has been weighed in the balance and found wanton.

Charlie was taking his out-of-town pal for a stroll through the city. The friend observed a goodlooking girl and asked Charlie if he knew her.

"Yes, that's Betty. Twenty dollars."

"How about that one?"

"That's Dolores. Forty dollars."

"Here comes one that's really first class. Do you know her?"

"That's Gloria. Eighty dollars."

"My God, aren't there any nice, respectable girls in this town?"

"Of course, but you couldn't afford their rates."

RACEHORSE: An animal that can take several thousand people for a ride at the same time.

Lester was continuously nervous and tense, so he went to his doctor. He was greeted by the lovely red-headed nurse, and he told her his problem. She said, "That's easy to fix." And she took him into a little room, relieved his tension, and said, "That will be ten dollars please."

A few weeks later he was nervous and tense again, went back to the doctor, and the doctor examined him and gave him a prescription for tranquilizers, and said, "That will be five dollars."

"If it's all the same to you, doc, I'd just as soon have the ten-dollar treatment."

Marriage starts with billing and cooing, but only the billing lasts.

A heartening note in women's fashions, of late, is that they're running truer to form.

There are more important things than money, but they won't date you if you don't have any.

It's easy to lie with a straight face, but it's nicer to lie with a curved body.

Margie was a newlywed, and after discussing the family budget with her husband, she decided she should get a temporary job. She went to the library and asked the old-maid librarian, "Could you please give me the name of a good book on positions?"

"What kind of positions did you have in mind?" asked the old librarian with a starched smile.

"Oh, you know," explained the bright-eyed young girl. "The different kinds of positions a bride might take."

An unemployed actor came home dejectedly after a day of fruitless job-hunting and found his wife lying on the bed with her clothes torn off, hysterical.

"Good Lord! Who did this to you?"

"Oh darling, I tried to fight him off. He came here looking for you and found me alone and defenseless."

"Who? Who did this awful thing?"

"Your agent."

"'My agent," he said, his face brightening, "Did he say whether he'd found a part for me?"

A sweater girl is one who knows that it's possible for a man to concentrate on two things at once.

MAD MONEY: A psychiatrist's fee.

The surest sign that a man is in love is when he divorces his wife.

When the struggling stenographer quits struggling, she often discovers she doesn't have to be a stenographer.

Max the plumber was summoned to a mansion to fix a leak, and tried to combine business with pleasure with the pretty maid. She refused on the grounds that her mistress was home and she didn't want to get fired. Next morning, she called him to say her mistress was out, and would he like to come over and see her.

"What!" yelled Max. "On my own time?"

Girls believe in love at first sight. Men believe in it at first opportunity.

In Rio on a business trip, Al was delighted when a lovely young girl sat down at his table in a restaurant.
"Do you speak English?" he asked.
"Si, bot jus' a leetle beet."
"Just a little bit, eh? How much?"
"Twenty-five dollars," was the prompt reply.

MISTRESS: A cutie on the Q.T.

If a girl expects to win a man, she has to exhibit a generous nature—or else how generous nature has been to her.

No matter how bad the movie at the drive-in theatre is, the patrons manage to love every minute of it.

Many a modern miss is known by the company that keeps her.

Census-takers have found that one tenth of all married couples aren't.

Nothing is more wasted than a smile on the face of a girl with a forty-inch bust.

Some girls make friends quickly. With strangers it takes a little longer.

Joe was out all night with a dazzling blonde. He came home at dawn and tried to appear quietly sober as his wife eyed him with suspicion.

"Joe, where's your underwear?" she said as he was undressing.

"My God," he cried with aggrieved dignity, "I've been robbed."

Card-playing can be expensive—but so can any game where you begin by holding hands.

Shapely limbs help many a girl to branch out.

The advance proofs of a cookbook for hipsters recently came our way. Wildest recipe is for a salad. You cut up lettuce, tomatoes, cucumbers, and green peppers. Then you add a dash of marijuana, and the salad tosses itself.

George and Charlie were in a steam bath, trying to get rid of last night's excess.

"How was your date last night?"

"Awful. Beautiful, but awful. The minute we got back to her apartment the phone started ringing, and we didn't have a moment's peace. Everybody in town was trying to get a date with her."

"Come on now. You expect a beautiful young girl to have her phone number listed in the phone book, don't you?"

"Yeah, but not in the Yellow Pages."

Muster some sympathy for the dilemma of the out-of-work stripteaser—all undressed and no place to show.

Give a man enough rope and he'll claim he's all tied up at the office.

An engaging, but somewhat vacant, young lady we met recently thought *vice versa* meant dirty poems.

When a boy is young, he thinks girls are made with sugar and spice, and everything nice. When he gets older, he discovers that it only takes sugar.

Some men don't give women a second thought. The first one covers everything.

The best kind of girl is one who says stop only when she sends a telegram.

PLATONIC FRIENDSHIP: What develops when two people grow tired of making love to each other.

One of the oldest, yet most perfect, examples of a redundant expression is the phrase "foolish virgins."

A really promiscuous girl is one you can have a good time with even if you play your cards wrong.

The three hundred passengers on the first fully automatic rocket plane flight from New York to Paris were aboard and belted in, and the great machine had whooshed aloft and into flight, when a voice came over the loudspeaker in measured tones of infinite assurance:

"Ladies and gentlemen, there is no crew on this aircraft, but there is nothing to worry about. Automation will fly you to Paris in perfect safety at a speed of twenty-five hundred miles per hour. Everything has been tested and retested so exhaustively for your safety that there is not the slightest chance anything can go wrong . . . GO WRONG . . . GO WRONG . . . GO WRONG. . . ."

Bow Wow: A TV performer's low-cut dress.

A career girl's mind moves her ahead, while a chorus girl's mind moves her behind.

Chivalry has changed from the days of Sir Walter Raleigh, but contrary to rumor, it hasn't died out altogether. A man will still lay his coat at the feet of a pretty girl; the difference is that now it's intended to keep her back from getting dirty.

Barry had just opened his law office, and immediately hired three goodlooking young stenographers to work for him.

"But how," a visiting friend inquired, eyeing the three, "do you expect to accomplish anything?"

"Simple. By giving two of them the day off."

"Come on baby, let's live for tonight," he said, making a play.

"Yes, but suppose we survive?"

BACHELOR: One who's footloose and fiancée free.

GOLD DIGGER: A girl who's got what it takes to take what you've got.

LOVER'S LEAP: The distance between twin beds.

MADAM: Someone for whom the belles toil.

SEX: The most fun you can have without laughing.

UNDERCOVER AGENT: A girl spy.

61

WINTER: The season of the year when gentlemen befur blondes.

ZOMBIE: Something some men drink and other men marry.

Just heard about the girl who was picked up so often she began to grow handles.

Martin was known among his friends for the punctuality with which he sent his wife her alimony payment each month. When asked the reason for his haste, he shivered and explained: "I'm afraid that if I ever should fall behind in my payments, she might decide to re-possess me."

We know a girl who was chased out of a nudist colony because she had something on her mind.

A girl who says she'll go through anything for a man usually has his bank account in mind.

"You can never tell about men," the sophisticated miss advised her younger sister. "Either they're so slow you want to scream, or so fast you have to."

Sam, a brilliant young inventor, had his living quarters and laboratory combined. A visitor was there, and Sam drew back the velvet curtains enclosing a cozy alcove. There, stretched out on the divan, was a beautiful nude blonde holding a glass, empty except for two ice cubes.

"This is my latest and greatest invention," Sam said. "I call it instant sex. You just add Scotch."

An empty-headed, lovely young girl stood at the bank teller's window. He looked at her and the check she wished to cash, then asked her if she could identify herself.

She pulled a small mirror from her handbag, glanced in it, and with relief said, "Yes, it's me all right."

It's usually a girl's geography that determines her history.

We know an amorous millionaire who's terribly indiscreet, yet so wealthy that he doesn't give a damn. He begins each letter to his sweethearts, "My darling, and gentlemen of the jury . . ."

NUDISTS: People who go in for altogetherness.

So seldom is she in her cups, Margie's forgotten what size she takes.

The inroads of television have trebled unemployment among film actors. Take the movie producer who came home unexpectedly one night and found his wife in the arms of one-time B-movie hero Chester Beefcake.

"Hey, what are you doing?"

"To tell you the truth, not much of anything else these days."

Marriage is a good deal like taking a bath—not so hot once you get accustomed to it.

Men who are getting on in years should console themselves with the thought that when they get too old to set bad examples, they can always start giving advice.

Gaston was explaining the plot of *Lolita* to Pierre. "It's an amazing book. It tells of a love affair between a middle-aged man and a twelve-year-old."
"Ah, a twelve-year-old *what?*"

VOLUPTUOUS WOMAN: One who has curves in places where some girls don't even have places.

A man said to his psychiatrist, "Doctor, you've got to help me. I'm sure I'm losing my mind. I can't remember anything, not what happened a year ago, or even what happened yesterday. I must be going crazy."
"How long have you had this problem?"
The man looked puzzled. "What problem?"

It was the first day for the new salesgirl at the maternity shop. It had been a hectic day; the store had been crowded from the moment the doors opened, and the girl had sped from one customer to another without stopping. Just as she anticipated a breathing spell, the doors opened and a fresh flood of expectant mothers poured in.

"Ye Gods," she cried, "doesn't anyone do it for fun any more?"

Many a man who thinks he's going on a maiden voyage with a girl finds out later from her lawyer that it was a shake-down cruise.

Shed a tear for the beatnik who committed suicide leaving a note saying, "Good-bye, cool world."

BACHELOR: A man who can take women or leave them, and prefers to do both.

When a girl is invited to a man's apartment to see his etchings, it's usually not a standing invitation.

Absent-minded is hardly the word for the pretty secretary who left her clothes at the office and took her boss to the cleaner.

Two advertising execs drinking their lunch and talking:
"Where has Charlie Harris been hanging out?"
"Haven't you heard? Charlie went to the great agency in the sky."
"Good Lord, you're kidding! What did he have?"
"Nothing much. A small toothpaste account and a couple of department stores, but nothing worth going after."

When a smart girl travels by train she gives the boys in the club car a wide berth.

A used-car dealer tells us that the usual standard sales pitch for a car that was owned by the little old lady who only used it on Sunday has been replaced by a nymphomaniac who only used the back seat.

The trouble with being kept is that the rent is always due.

Two mothers talking:
"It's really none of my business, but have you noticed what your daughter is up to?"
"Why no. What is it?"
"She's knitting tiny garments."
"Well, thank goodness. I'm glad to see she's taken an interest in something besides running around with boys."

OLD AGE: A time when a man sees a pretty girl and it arouses his memory instead of his hopes.

When the sweet young thing found out that the handsome young millionaire was fond of hunting, she told him she was game.

ANATOMY: Something that everybody has, but it looks better on a girl.

BORE: A guy with a cocktail glass in one hand and your lapel in the other.

COOPERATION: An exchange between a woman and a man in which she coos and he operates.

GOOD CLEAN FUN: A couple taking a bath together.

HUSBAND: A poor unfortunate who began by handing out a line and ended by walking it.

KISS: Application for a better position.

A girl who finds it possible to resist every attempt to
seduce her should be going out with stronger men.

A Word to the Weight-Conscious: If you want to get a youthful figure, ask a woman her age.

A pretty young girl stretched out on the psychiatrist's couch.

"I just can't help myself, doctor. No matter how hard I try to resist, I bring five or six men with me into my bedroom every night. Last night there were ten. I just feel so miserable, I don't know what to do."

In understanding tones, the doctor rumbled, "Yes, I know, I know my dear."

"Oh," the surprised girl exclaimed, "were you there last night too?"

We know a man who thinks marriage is a fifty-fifty proposition, which convinces us that he doesn't understand women or percentages.

You never know how a girl will turn out until her folks turn in.

SALESMANSHIP: The difference between rape and rapture.

They moved apart as Frank lit their cigarettes. Then she snuggled close to him again and pulled the bedsheets up around their chins.

"Darling," she cooed, "how many others were there before me?"

After a few minutes of silence, she said, with a slight pout, "Well, I'm still waiting."

"Well," he replied, puffing thoughtfully, "I'm still counting."

The nightclub's hat-check girl was obviously new, and Jack watched in amusement while she fumbled to find his coat and knocked garments off the racks and entangled herself in the hangers. His amusement changed to fury, however, when a quarter of an hour later she had still not found his coat.

"Forget it," he finally cried in rage, "I'll send someone for it tomorrow." Seething, he walked out into the cold.

"Hey, you cheapskate," she called, "what about my tip?"

Some people have no respect for age unless it's bottled.

Everybody thought the Miss Albuquerque Beauty Contest was going to be a hotly contested affair, but Susan walked away with first place with nary a dissenting vote. She was the only one of the contestants who could get all those letters across her chest.

This year's college graduates deserve your sympathy. Almost anywhere they look for work, they run a terrible risk of finding it.

It's no fun to kiss a girl over the phone unless you happen to be in the same room with her.

Florence and Emily, two pretty young housewives, arranged to have cocktails and lunch together. When they met, Emily could see that something serious was bothering her friend.

"Come on, out with it. What's depressing you?"

"I'm ashamed to admit it, but I caught my husband making love."

"Why let that bother you? I got mine the same way."

The reason today's girls will do things their mothers wouldn't think of doing is that their mothers didn't think of doing them.

It's easy to admire a good loser at a strip poker party.

NEUROTIC: A person who worries about things that didn't happen in the past, instead of worrying about something that won't happen in the future, like normal people.

A girl should use what Mother Nature gave her before Father Time takes it away.

Many an actress' career begins when she becomes too
big for her sweaters and ends when she becomes too big
for her britches.

Latest word from Hollywood concerns a young producer moving into lavish new offices who had his interior decorator on the carpet because she'd forgotten to include a studio couch.

The gods gave man fire, and he invented fire engines. They gave him love, and he invented marriage.

Charlie entered the airline ticket office, and the girl behind the counter was as magnificently endowed with feminine equipment as any girl he could ever remember seeing. She was wearing a low cut dress and bending low over notations she was making. He stared at her.

She looked up, and said, "What can I do for you, sir?"

Charlie heard his own breath hissing in his ears like steam, but tried to master the situation. He did, after all, need two tickets to Pittsburgh. He finally spoke.

"Uh, give me two pickets to . . . ."

Pitiable is the word for Milton the manufacturer. He accumulated millions, making men's suits, and lost it all, making one skirt.

As soon as most women have a drink or two, they start looking for a chaser.

TAXPAYERS: People who don't have to pass civil service examinations in order to work for the government.

To most modern writers, sex is a novel idea.

Mark fixed himself a Martini, while waiting for Peggy to get ready for their date. She came out of the shower, wrapped in a bath towel, and said, "I'm sorry I'm late, but I was shopping and lost track of the time. Would you like to see me in my new dress?"
He smiled, "I would like *nothing* better."

We find ourselves in complete accord with the etiquette expert who says that only well-reared girls should wear slacks.

Some women, like prizefighters, won't go into action until they see a ring.

When a girl says she's got a boyish figure, it's usually straight from the shoulder.

A friend of ours has come up with the David and Goliath Cocktail. A small one, and you're stoned.

A man approached a beautiful young girl in a bar, and said, "You know, I hate to see a young girl like you ruin her reputation and destroy her character by hanging around a bar. Let me take you someplace where the atmosphere is quiet and more refined, like my apartment."

NEUROTIC: A woman who likes a psychiatrist's couch better than a double bed.

Men with money to burn have started many a girl playing with fire.

Advice to the Exhausted: When wine, women and song become too much for you, give up singing.

If all the world loves a lover, why do they have hotel detectives?

Pierre, the passionate masseur, was recently fired when he rubbed a lady customer the wrong way.

Sometimes a girl can attract a man by her mind, but more often she can attract him by what she doesn't mind.

79

When Harry returned, looking tanned and rested, his secretary asked him about his vacation.

"Well," he replied, "a friend of mine invited me up to his hunting lodge, a quiet, secluded place. No night life, no parties, not a woman within a hundred miles."

"Did you enjoy yourself?" she asked.

"Who went?" he said.

There's a secret method for returning from Las Vegas with a small fortune. Go with a large fortune.

"Georgie, will you love me always?"

"Certainly, darling. Which way would you like me to try first?"

INTELLECTUAL GIRL: One who can think up excuses that her boyfriend's wife will believe.

An executive friend of ours is so dedicated to his work that he keeps his secretary near his bed in case he gets an idea during the night.

A model we know says she's looking for a man who can fill a void in her life—an empty clothes closet.

JURY: A group of twelve people selected to decide who has the better lawyer.

One thing that can be said in favor of going steady is that it gets the youngsters home and in bed at an early hour.

A man of sixty-four who had just married a girl less than half his age went to his doctor for a check-up.

"Well, doc, do you think I'm overweight?" he asked after the examination.

"No, just over-matched."

Girls' dresses have gotten so short we wonder what the designers will be up to next.

He'd shown her his etchings and poured her another martini.

"Tell me," he said, "do you object to making love?"

"That's something I've never done," she said.

"Never made love?"

"No, silly. Never objected."

APPETIZERS: Little things you eat until you lose your appetite.

It's hard to keep a good girl down, but lots of fun trying.

The lingerie manufacturer was trying to talk the TV M.C. into plugging his product.

"Listen, how would you like to plug my product on your show?"

"That all depends on what's in it for me."

"I'll send you one of our finest and flimsiest negligees. How's that?"

"That all depends on what's in it for me."

The newspaper account of George's tragic death read: "His friends could give no reason why he should have committed suicide. He was a bachelor."

"You know, you're the first man I've met whose kisses make me sit up and open my eyes."
"Really?"
"Yes, usually they have the opposite effect."

Two heads are better than one, especially if they happen to be on the same coin.

A good resolution is like many a pretty modern girl. Easy to make but hard to keep.

RACE TRACK: A place where windows clean people.

The censors of the cinema have never given proper credit to a group probably more responsible than any other for keeping sex out of the movies: ushers.

Two expectant fathers paced the floor in the waiting room of the hospital.
"What tough luck," said one. "This had to happen during my vacation."

"You think you've got troubles," said the other. "I'm on my honeymoon."

Latest invention we heard about is a toothpaste with built-in food particles for people who can't eat between every brushing.

NUDISM: A different way of looking at things.

The boss listened to the young man ask for a raise, then said, "Sylvester, I know you can't get married on the salary I'm paying you—and some day you'll thank me for it."

Some girls are discreet up to a point, and some are discreet up to a pint.

Harry took a beautiful but very brainless girl up to his apartment. She looked with perplexed eyes at his books and paintings, then, pointing to a carved wooden object on the mantle, asked, "What in the world is that thing?"

"Oh, that's African. It was used in fertility rites. Actually, it's a phallic symbol."

"Well," she said, "I'd hate to tell you what it looks like."

A husband came home, and found his wife in bed
with his best friend.

"See here! What do you think you're doing?"

"See?" she said to the man beside her. "I told you he
was stupid."

Women are the kind of problem most men like to wrestle with.

The reason no one ever gives the groom a shower is that everyone figures him to be washed up anyway.

CAD: A man who refuses to help his date with the breakfast dishes.

If the birth rate keeps increasing, there will be standing room only on the earth, in which case the birth rate should stop increasing pretty quickly.

A girl with an hourglass figure can often make grown men feel like playing in the sand.

We've come across a refreshingly unique proposal of marriage: "Honey, how would you like to do this *every* night?"

The dictionary defines both bigamy and marriage as having one wife too many.

HULA DANCE: A shake in the grass.

INDIVIDUALIST: A man who lives in the city and commutes to the suburbs.

ORGY: Group therapy.

WELL-PROPORTIONED GIRL: One with a narrow waist and a broad mind.

Sign at the entrance of a nudist's colony: "PLEASE BARE WITH US."

Girls who don't repulse men's advances advance men's pulses.

The difference between a wife and a mistress is night and day.

Whether or not a girl in a rented bathing suit attracts a lot of attention depends on where the rent is.

While they were crushed together in a passionate embrace, he decided to tell her.

"Honey," he said, "I want you to know that I think

you're a wonderful person, but as far as I'm concerned, wedlock is out of the question."

In reply, she moved closer and uttered a small sigh of pleasure.

"I mean," he continued, "you're more like a sister to me."

"My God," she murmured, "what a home life you must have."

Marriage is like a long banquet with the dessert served first.

After a pleasant picnic in the woods, Mark described his girlfriend as the down-to-earth type.

The lady's French maid was leaving to get married. She said, "Juliette, I am overjoyed for you. You will have it much easier now that you're getting married."

"Yes madam, and more frequently as well."

Hollywood marriages are evidently losing their reputation for brevity. We've heard about a producer who liked one of his wives so well he decided to hold her over for a second week.

To most couples, curbing their emotions means parking.

The young bride was having her new house deco-
rated, and she noticed where her husband had left a
hand print on a freshly painted wall. She slipped into a
flimsy negligee, and called the painter who was working downstairs.

"Pardon me, but would you like to see where my husband put his hand last night?"

"I'd love to, lady, but I've got to get done with this
painting first."

Whether or not a girl can be had for a song depends on the man's pitch.

EXPERIENCE: The wonderful knowledge that enables you to recognize a mistake when you make it again.

A wife made to order can't compare with a ready maid.

Anxious to be on time for his date, Carl stopped at the drug store for a hasty purchase. The druggist gave him a knowing smile, and he told the druggist about a lovely chick he met at a party. He was going to spend the evening with her, and her parents would be out at the opera.

When he got to her house, she and her mother were waiting for her father to return from work.

When her father walked in, she introduced both parents to Carl, and Carl said, "Say, why don't Nancy and I join you this evening?"

"You children don't want to spend your evening with us old folks," said Nancy's mother.

"Sure we do," said Carl.

"I didn't know you liked opera," the bewildered Nancy said to her date, as he was helping her on with her coat.

"No, and I didn't know your father was a druggist either," he said.

MANIC-DEPRESSIVE: A person whose philosophy is: easy glum, easy glow.

The reason the modern girl's bathing suit is real cool is that most of it is real gone.

A millionaire we know has filled his swimming pool with Martinis. He claims it's impossible to drown, since the deeper you sink, the higher you get.

Girls who think they will hate themselves in the morning should learn to sleep till noon.

One of the recent cases investigated by the Director of Internal Revenue was that of a young girl who listed her apartment rent as "expenses incurred while entertaining clients."

"Hey, Sally, how come you're not wearing my fraternity pin?"
"It was such a nuisance. All the fellows were complaining that it scratched their hands."

George was describing his new secretary enthusiastically to his family.

"She's efficient, personable, clever, punctual, and darned attractive. In short, she's a real doll."

At which point their five-year-old daughter, who knew about dolls, looked up and said, "And does she close her eyes when you lay her down, daddy?"

Business was brisk for the pretty little call girl at the bar.

"Bill, you can come over about seven-ish, and you, George, around eight-ish, and Frank, I'll have time for you about nine-ish."

She looked around the crowded bar.

"Ten-ish, anyone?"

"Oh, you'll like it here," said the experienced steno to the new girl. "Lots of chances for advances."

"It was terrible, Mother, I had to change my seat four times at the movie."

"You mean some man started bothering you?"

"Yes—finally."

At the inquest, the widow was asked if she could remember her late husband's last words.

"Yes. He said, 'I don't see how they make a profit out of this stuff at a dollar and a quarter a fifth.' "

We know a girl who started out with a little slip and ended up with a whole new wardrobe.

The traveling salesman asked the farmer to put him up for the night. The farmer said, "Sure, but you'll have to sleep with my son."

"Good Lord," said the salesman, "I'm in the wrong joke."

The six fraternity men came weaving out of the off-campus gin mill. The president said to one of the fellows, "Herbie, you drive. You're too drunk to sing."

HIGH FIDELITY: A drunk who goes home regularly to his wife.

The ideal wife would be a beautiful, sex-starved deaf mute who owns a liquor store.

"Oh, doctor, do you mean I'm cured of my kleptomania? I don't know how I can ever repay you."

"My fee is the only payment I expect. However, if you should happen to have a relapse, you might pick me up a small transistor radio."

The meek little bank clerk had his suspicions. One day he left work early, and sure enough, when he arrived home, he found a strange hat and umbrella in the hallway and his wife on the couch in the arms of another man.

Wild for revenge, the husband picked up the man's umbrella and snapped it in two across his knee.

"There. Now I hope it rains."

There was an area of disagreement between the young bachelor and the sexy widow. He had sired the latest addition to her brood, and they went to court. The judge asked him, "Did you sleep with this woman?"

"No, your honor. Not a wink."

We asked a zoologist how porcupines have sex.

"Carefully, very carefully."

Trouble with being the best man at the wedding is that you don't get a chance to prove it.

The analyst was concerned about the results of a Rorschach test he had just given for the patient who associated every ink blot with some sort of sexual activity.

"I want to study the results of your test over the week-end, and I'd like to see you Monday," he said to the patient.

"Okay, doc. I'm going to a stag party tomorrow night. Any chance I might borrow those dirty pictures of yours?"

Staggering into his apartment, the bibber deposited himself on the bed and fell asleep. An hour later, he was awakened by a knock at the door. He staggered out of bed and opened it to find his drinking companion of the evening.

"Gee, I'm sorry to wake you up, Joe."

"Oh, that's all right. I had to get up to answer the door anyway."

The Internal Revenue Department has streamlined its tax form for this year. It goes like this: (A) How much did you make last year? (B) How much have you left? (C) Send B.

A newspaperman was interviewing the sixty-five-year-old rodeo champion.

"You're really an extraordinary man to be a rodeo champ at sixty-five."

"Heck, I'm not nearly the man my pa is. He was just signed to play guard for a pro football team, and he's eighty-eight. He's in Fort Worth now, standing up to my grandpa's wedding. My grandpa's 114."

"Amazing," said the newspaper man. "You're a rodeo champ at sixty-five, your father's a football player at eighty-eight, and now your grandfather wants to get married at 114."

"Hell, mister, grandpa doesn't *want* to get married. He *has* to."

Henry was trying to help his son fly a kite in the back yard, but couldn't get it to stay in the air. His wife called from the back door, "Henry, you need more tail."

"I wish you'd make up your mind. Last night you told me to go fly a kite."

The expectant father was talking to a relaxed veteran father in the waiting room of the maternity ward.

"This is our first child. How long after the baby is born can you resume marital relations with your wife?"

"Well, that depends on whether she's in a ward or a private room."

An ornithologist says that the stork is too often held responsible for circumstances which might be better attributed to a lark.

ADULT WESTERN: One in which the hero still loves his horse, only now he's worried about it.

101

The gentleman in the upper berth was awakened by a persistent tapping from below.

"I'm terribly cold down here. I wonder if you would mind getting me a blanket," said a lady's voice.

"I have a better idea," he said sleepily. "Let's pretend we're married."

"That sounds like a lovely idea," she giggled.

"Good," he said rolling over. "Now go get your own damn blanket."

"I understand you took out that gorgeous new receptionist last night. How was she?"

"Not so good."

"Yeah, you always were lucky."

The handsome young man walked over to the beautiful girl sitting at the end of the bar.

"You must forgive my rudeness, but you're so beautiful I had to speak to you," he said. "I've never gazed upon such beauty before. I want to lay Manhattan at your feet, buy you jewels, exotic perfumes, and a thousand other wondrous things. If you bid me welcome, we will fly this very night to Paris, then on to Venice,

Rome, India, and finally Egypt for a trip down the Nile."

She was utterly taken with this handsome stranger, and could only manage a breathless "Yes."

"Then go prepare yourself, my Juliet, my Venus, my Helen of Troy. When you are ready, call me at the number on this card. My Rolls Royce will come for you and take you to my plane."

"Is this your private number at your town house or country estate?" she asked.

"Well," he said, "it's actually the delicatessen downstairs, but they'll call me."

Relatives of the late millionaire were gathered for the reading of the will, and at the far corner of the room was seated the curvey blonde who had served as his secretary for the past two years.

"And finally, to Miss Simpson, my beautiful but unfortunately uncooperative secretary, whom I promised to remember here: Hello there, Miss Simpson."

Most girls wouldn't stay out late if fellows didn't make them.

Mary and Bob were in their upper berth on the train to Niagara Falls, and she kept repeating, "Bobby, I just can't believe that we're really married."

From the lower berth bellowed a sleepy voice, "For Chrissake, Bobby, convince her—we wanna get to sleep."

A woman with a past attracts men who hope history will repeat itself.

A divorce case was in process, and the wealthy woman complained to the judge that her husband had left her bed and board.

He rose and said, "Correction, Your Honor, I left her bed—bored."

"I had everything a man could want," mooned a sad-eyed friend of ours. "Money, a handsome home, the love of a beautiful and wealthy woman. Then, bang, one morning my wife walked in!"

Never pour black coffee into an intoxicated person. If you do, you'll wind up with a wide-awake drunk on your hands.

Conversation at the club had turned to sex and the techniques thereof.

"But should I talk to my wife while making love?" asked newly-wed Fred.

"Certainly," counseled an older member, "if you happen to be near a phone."

Two little Hollywood boys were exchanging taunts.
"My father can beat your father."
"Oh, yeah? My father *is* your father."

Many a wife thinks her husband is the world's greatest lover. But she can never manage to catch him at it.

Harry constantly irritated his friends with his eternal optimism. No matter how bad the situation, he would always say, "It could have been worse."

To cure him of this annoying habit, his friends decided to invent a situation so completely black, so dreadful, that even Harry could find no hope in it. Approaching him at the club bar one day, one of them said, "Harry! did you hear what happened to George? He came home last night, found his wife in bed with another man, shot them both, then turned the gun on himself!"

"Terrible," said Harry. "But it could have been worse."

"How in hell," asked his dumbfounded friend, "could it possibly have been worse?"

"Well," said Harry, "if it had happened the night before, I'd be dead now."

"If I refuse to go to bed with you," she whispered, will you really commit suicide?"

"That," he said grandly, "has been my usual procedure."

After rushing into a drugstore, the nervous young man was obviously embarrassed when a prim, middle-aged woman asked if she could serve him.

"No-no," he stammered, "I'd rather see the druggist."

"I'm the druggist," she responded cheerfully. "What can I do for you?"

"Oh . . . well, uh, it's nothing important," he said, and turned to leave.

"Young man," said the woman, "my sister and I have been running this drugstore for nearly thirty years. There is nothing you can tell us that will embarrass us."

"Well, all right," he said. "I have this awful sexual hunger that nothing will appease. No matter how many times I make love, I still want to make love again. Is there anything you can give me for it?"

"Just a moment," said the little lady, "I'll have to discuss this with my sister."

A few minutes later she returned. "The best we can offer," she said, "is $200 a week and half-interest in the business."

In a whiskey it's age, in a cigarette it's taste, and in a sports car it's impossible.

An Easterner on business in Kentucky met a young
lady in a bar, and invited her to his room. As she was
disrobing, he said, "Say, how old are you?"

"Thirteen."

"Thirteen? My God! You get those clothes back on
and get out of here."

Pausing briefly at the door, the perplexed nymphet
said, "Superstitious, huh?"

Despite warnings from his guide, an American skiing in Switzerland got separated from his group and fell—uninjured—into a deep crevasse. Several hours later, a rescue party found the yawning pit, and to reassure the stranded skier, shouted down to him, "We're from the Red Cross!"

"Sorry," the imperturbable American echoed back, "I already gave at the office!"

Our Unabashed Dictionary defines the difference between picnic and panic as twenty-eight days.

Who says the dieting craze is wearing thin? We know a guy whose girlfriend told him that if it wasn't for Metrecal she wouldn't be able to get into her toreador pants. So he's been drinking the stuff ever since.

Moving along a dimly lighted street, a friend of ours was suddenly approached by a stranger who had slipped from the shadows nearby.

"Please, sir," asked the stranger, "would you be so kind as to help a poor unfortunate fellow who is hungry and out of work? All I have in the world is this gun."

Boasting Sam, one of the worst braggarts who ever bent a bar rail, was loudly lamenting that his doctor had ordered him to give up half of his sex life.

"Which half are you going to give up?" asked a weary listener. "Talking about it or thinking about it?"

A Madison Avenue friend of ours tells of a client who wanted to get his "message" to every married woman in a specific community. The solution to the problem was simple, according to this enterprising publicist: "We just addressed letters to every married man in town, and marked them 'Personal.'"

Have you heard about the new insecticide that, while it doesn't actually kill flies, makes them so sexy that you can swat them two at a time?

Sign in a pharmacy window: "FOR THE GIRL WHO HAS EVERYTHING—PENICILLIN."

"Police?" came the voice on the phone. "I want to report a burglar trapped in an old maid's bedroom!" After ascertaining the address, the police sergeant asked who was calling.

"This," cried the frantic voice, "is the burglar!"

With deep concern, Dick noted that his friend Con-
rad was drunker than he'd ever seen him before.

"What's the trouble, buddy?"

"It's a woman."

"Tell me about it."

"It's your wife."

"My wife? What about her?"

"Well, buddy-boy, I'm afraid she's cheating on us."

Sometimes when two's company, three's the result.

The pretty young thing came slamming into her apartment after a blind date and announced to her roommate, "Boy, what a character! I had to slap his face three times this evening!"

The roommate inquired eagerly, "What did he do?"

"Nothing," muttered the girl. "I slapped him to see if he was awake!"

A stunningly stacked blonde walked into a dress shop, and asked the manager, "I wonder if I might try on that blue dress in the window?"

"Go right ahead," he said. "It might help business."

Then there was the band leader who spent all week working on a new arrangement and then discovered that his wife wasn't going out of town after all.

The bank robbers arrived just before closing and promptly ordered the few remaining depositors, the tellers, clerks, and guards to disrobe and lie, face down, behind the counter. One nervous blonde pulled off her clothes and lay down on the floor, facing upwards.

"Turn over, Maybelle," whispered the girl lying beside her, "this is a stick-up, not an office party."

113

The newly appointed chairman of the local fund-raising committee decided to call personally at the home of the town's wealthiest citizen, a man well known for his tightness with a dollar. Remarking on the impressive economic resources of his host, the committee chairman pointed out how miserly it would seem if the town's richest man failed to give a substantial donation to the annual charity drive.

"Since you've gone to so much trouble checking on my assets," the millionaire retorted, "let me fill you in on some facts you may have overlooked. I have a ninety-one-year-old mother who has been hospitalized for the past five years, a widowed daughter with five young children and no means of support, and two brothers who owe the Government a fortune in back taxes. Now, I think you'll agree, young man, that charity begins at home."

Ashamed for having misjudged his host, the fund raiser apologized for his tactlessness and added, "I had no idea that you were saddled with so many family debts."

"I'm not," replied the millionaire, "but you must be crazy to think I'd give money to strangers when I won't even help my own relatives."

Our Unabashed Dictionary defines minute man as a fellow who double-parks in front of a house of ill repute.

Have you heard what they call uncircumcised Jewish babies? Girls.

Some men are so interested in their wives' continued happiness that they hire detectives to find out the reason for it.

Las Vegas is a great place to go to get tanned and faded at the same time.

A lovely young thing entered a doctor's office on her lunch hour, and addressed a handsome young man in a white coat.

"I've had a pain in my shoulder for a week. Can you help me?" she asked.

"Lie down on this table," he said, "and I'll massage it for you."

After a few minutes, the beautiful patient exclaimed, "Doctor, that isn't my shoulder!"

The young man smiled, and replied: "No, and I'm not a doctor, either."

While making the rounds of producers' and casting directors' offices, Sally made a successful contact, and as a result, was offered a speaking role in a feature-length western.

The first day's script called for her to be thrown from a horse into a clump of cacti. The second day, she had to jump from a cliff, her clothes on fire, into a mountain stream, and swim to shore. On the third day, she was cuffed around by the villain, and the director—a stickler for realism—reshot the scene five times. The fourth day, her boot caught in a stirrup, and a runaway horse dragged her two miles.

She managed to limp wearily to the producer's office.

"Listen," she said hoarsely, "Who do I have to sleep with to get *out* of this picture?"

The young executive greeted his attractive secretary warmly as he entered the office.

"Good morning, Marge," he said, tossing his briefcase on his desk. "I had a dream about you last night."

Flattered, but wishing to appear aloof, she casually inquired, "Oh, did you?"

"No," her boss replied. "I woke up too soon."

Then there was the fellow who got badly scratched up fighting for his girl's honor. She wanted to keep it.

In the presence of a client he wished to impress, a high-powered executive flipped on his intercom switch, and barked to his secretary: "Miss Jones, get my broker!"

The visitor was duly impressed, until the secretary's voice floated back into the room, loud and clear: "Yes, sir, stock or pawn?"

The theatrical agent, trying to sell a new strip act to a night-club manager, was raving about the girl's unbelievable 72-26-40 figure.

"What kind of a dance does she do?" the manager

asked, duly impressed by the description of the girl's dimensions.

"Well, she doesn't actually dance at all," the agent replied. "She just crawls out onto the stage and tries to stand up!"

A sexy blonde with a stunning figure boarded a bus and, finding no vacant seats, asked a gentleman for his, explaining that she was pregnant. The man stood up at once and gave her his seat, but couldn't help commenting that she didn't look pregnant.

"Well," she replied with a smile, "it's only been about half an hour."

Two successful big-business executives met at a trade convention.

"Tell me," said one, "how's business?"

"Well, you know how it is," replied the other. "My line is like sex. When it's good, it's wonderful—and when it's bad, it's still pretty good!"

The popularity of TV Westerns is even influencing milady's dainty underthings: There's a new brassiere on the market that is patterned after television's "Rawhide"—it rounds 'em up and heads 'em out.

Two little boys were engaging in the traditional verbal battle of little boys everywhere:

"My father is better than your father."

"No he's not."

"My brother is better than your brother."

"No he's not."

"My mother is better than your mother."

"Well, I guess you've got me there. My father says the same thing."

A man brings his boss home for dinner. A woman lets them in the front door. The boss asks, "Was that your wife?"

"Would I have a maid that ugly?" answers the man.

A woman walks into a pet shop and sees a bird with a big beak.

"What's that strange-looking bird?" she asks the proprietor.

"That's a gobble bird," he answers.

"Why do you call him a gobble bird?"

The man says to the bird, "Gobble bird my chair."

The bird immediately starts pecking away and gobbles up the chair.

"I'll buy him," the woman says.

The owner asks why.

"Well," she says, "when my husband comes home, he'll see the bird and ask, 'What's that?' I'll say, 'A gobble bird.' Then he'll say, 'Gobble bird my foot!'"

MADISON AVENUE EXECUTIVE: One who takes the padding out of his shoulders and puts it on his expense account.

SLIP COVER: A maternity dress.

Almost as pitiable as the fellow who was tried and found wanting is the guy who wanted and was found trying.

Generally speaking, women are.

When Cleo's parents threatened to forbid her to see her boyfriend unless she told them why he'd been there so late the night before, she began to talk.
"Well, I took him him into the loving room, and . . ."
"That's *living*, dear," said her mother.
"You're telling me!"

These days, the necessities of life cost you about three times what they used to, and half the time you find they aren't even fit to drink.

"O.K., you're hired," said the busy executive, moving around his desk toward the buxom young female. "Now, would you like to try for a raise?"

A girl with a well-developed sense of fashion realizes that bare skin never clashes with anything she's wearing.

In the new jet planes, you know you're moving faster than sound when the stewardess slaps your face before you can get a word out.

History credits Adam and Eve with being the first bookkeepers, because they invented the first loose-leaf system.

A man who looked like a high-powered executive began to drop in at Milton's Bar regularly, and his order was always the same—two Martinis. After several weeks of this, Milton asked him why he didn't order a double instead.

"It's a sentimental thing," he said. "A very dear friend of mine died a few weeks ago, and before his death he asked that when I drink I have one for him too."

A week later the customer came in and ordered one Martini.

"What about your dead buddy? Why only one Martini today?"

"This is my buddy's drink. I'm on the wagon."

VOLUME THREE

Henny Youngman's Bar Bets, Bar Jokes

illustrated

Frontispiece: Caricature by Anthony D'Adamo

To my wife Sadie,
the J.A.P. (Jewish-American Princess).
To my son Gary,
the Film Editor.
To my brother Lester,
(I wish he'd get a job so we'd know
what kind of work he's always out of!)
To my daughter Marilyn.
And to my grandson Larry Kelly,
who's seventeen and is going to be
eighteen if I let him. He's always complaining about headaches. I've told him
a thousand times, "When you get out
of bed, it's feet first!"

NOW TAKE THIS BOOK.......PLEASE!

...But First, PAY FOR IT!

You are sitting at a bar and you'd really love to strike up a conversation with that beautiful blonde! You are trying to get that stone-faced buyer to smile, at a business meeting! You are sitting at a dull party (at your own house, no less!) and you want everyone to get to know each other better! Or you are with the boys at the corner pub and you want to win a few free drinks (after all, payday isn't until Friday)!

O.K.! Step in a bit closer...you came to the right place!

That's why I am dedicating this collection of "Bar Bets, Bar Jokes, Bar Tricks" to you!

If you are a quiet, normal, level-headed human being, you usually avoid "baggy pants comedy" and a "Mr. Show Biz" attitude. But under all that calm exterior and even disposition lurks a bit of Hollywood and Broadway, all rolled into one. Everyone of us dreams of being a guest on the TV talk show or playing the "Big Room" at the Dunes or the T-Bird in Las Vegas (Me too, me too!).

Well, take my advice, go back to your job...stay in school...and don't come to New York....Do you think I want *competition?* What I mean to say is, read the book, try out some of these puzzles and stunts when the occasion arises, and you just might become the center of attraction . . . you might pick up a few free drinks (of Coke, of course!), and that beautiful blonde may just give you a second glance (the rest is up to you . . . I'm a happily married man!).

RULES OF THE HOUSE

All of these "bar bits" have been gathered from collections dating back over one hundred years (sounds like Milton Berle's gagfile!). They have all been written in the form of wagers, bets or challenges. They appear to be difficult and some are, until the secret is revealed (which you don't; until you have won the game!). You use them as "ice-breakers," as simple games, or demonstrate them as "magic tricks." Your kids and your old-maid aunt will not be offended by them, as not one of these bets is off-color or in bad taste (some are a bit wacky, of course!). Keep the bet small, since some of the solutions to the stunts are a bit "far out," and some are just jokes made for laffs! Make sure your buddy is a good sport *before* you attempt the stunt, otherwise you risk the consequences of a "fist sandwich!"

And remember, all of the stunts are "just for fun" and should be presented in a light-hearted manner. Avoid a wise-guy, "the joke's on you" attitude which will defeat the entertainment value for your "audience." Who knows, they may start a fan club in your honor if they like you!

All of the bets use simple items like coins, matches and glasses; all found at home or at a lounge. Toothpicks or pretzel sticks may be substituted for matches. Sugar cubes, olives or "odds 'n' ends" may be used in

Foreword

place of coins (Remember . . . payday, Friday!). Make everything nice and easy for yourself by preparing your "props" before you plan to "go on"! Do not, I repeat, do *not* force these stunts on your friends! Wait until the right moment to perform, when they will fully appreciate your "artistry."

Then remember, go back to your job, stay in school and above all, stay out of show business. . . . I need every dollar I can get!

HENNY

Henny Youngman's
Bar Bets

EGG CREAM

Bet that you can make an egg float on water. When all bets are covered, put the egg in a glass of water, and add loads of salt until the egg rises to the top.

EGG BALANCE

Ask everyone to try to balance an egg on end. When they fail, you can make the egg stand upright.

Secretly, before the bet is made, place some salt under the tablecloth. Stand the egg large end down over the salt, which helps to balance it.

STRONG THUMB

Have someone sit in a chair with his face looking up at the ceiling. Press your thumb hard on the center of his forehead above the bridge of the nose. Challenge him to rise out of the chair without using his hands. It is quite difficult, if not impossible!

MONEY MAKER

Tell everyone to lay quarters heads down on a table. State that *you are willing to pay a dime for every quarter* whose date you can't name, sight unseen.

The more dates you fail to guess, the better you are. Because at the end, you pick up the quarters one by one and hand each owner a dime instead.

Remind them that you said, *"I will pay a dime for every quarter* whose date I couldn't name. I'm paying dimes for quarters."

SOMETHING FOR NOTHING

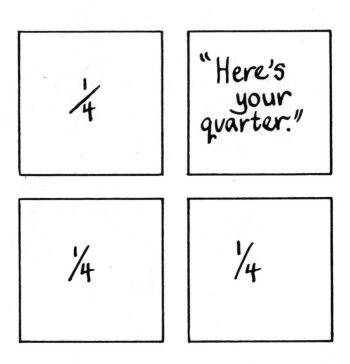

Bet someone that if he can tear a sheet of paper into four equal pieces, you will give him a quarter.

Naturally, anyone can come close to tearing the sheet into four equal pieces. So hand him a *quarter* (one of the four pieces of paper).

A quarter of the paper, right?

FIRE AND WATER

Bet that you can make water run up hill.

Pour water into a plate. Drop a burning piece of paper into a glass, and immediately invert the glass with the burning paper, and put it mouth down into the water-filled plate.

As the flame goes out, a vacuum forms and pulls the water up into the glass!

WHISKEY AND WATER

Fill one whiskey glass with whiskey and another with water. Challenge your barmates to transpose the water and whiskey without touching either liquid!

Here's how. Place a small square of cardboard (business card or playing card will do) on the glass of water. Holding the card to the glass to form a vacuum, turn the glass of water over and place it in this inverted position on top of the glass of whiskey with the card between.

Now, move the card slightly, so air is permitted to pass along one edge of the glass and over the edge of the card. *The two liquids will switch places!*

TAILS YOU LOSE

Place any coin, heads up, under a glass and cover the glass with a handkerchief. Bet that you can turn the coin tails-up without picking up the glass. Have someone place their hand on the handkerchief over the glass to prevent you from lifting it.

Now place your hand under the handkerchief and give the glass a slight turn. Remove the coin, and say, "It is done. Let's see if I win." As soon as they remove the handkerchief and lift the glass, immediately reach over and turn the coin tails-up, and say, "See, I win! I didn't lift the cup, you did!"

WET BET

Fill a glass of water or liquid right up to the brim.

Place your bets as to how many coins can go into the water before the liquid spills over. All coin bets are dropped carefully, one at a time, into the glass. Many additional coins can be added before it spills over as the liquid swells up over the top of the glass rim.

HARD WATER

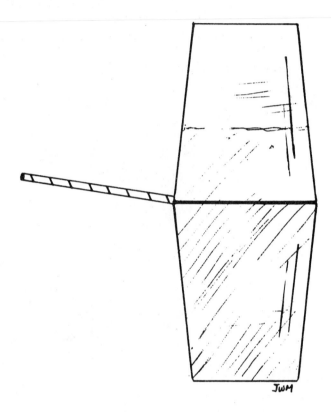

JWM

Fill a glass of water to the brim. Fill a second glass to the brim, and place a piece of stiff paper over the mouth of the second glass and invert it. The water does not fall out, even though the glass is upside-down.

Now place the inverted glass on top of the other,

mouth to mouth. Pull the paper out slowly.

Now bet that you can drink all the water out of the top glass without lifting it off.

The secret is to place a drinking straw at the line where the rims meet and drink until all the water in the top glass is consumed.

THREE MATCHES

Borrow a quarter. Place it on the table and lay three matches around it, triangle fashion. Then bet a dime that they won't answer "three matches" to each of three questions.

First ask two ordinary questions to which the bettor will answer "three matches." Then ask "What will you take for your quarter?" If he says "three matches," give him the three matches and a dime (He wins the bet but loses fifteen cents).

If he won't say "three matches," he gets his quarter back, but he loses the dime bet.

CATCH A BUCK

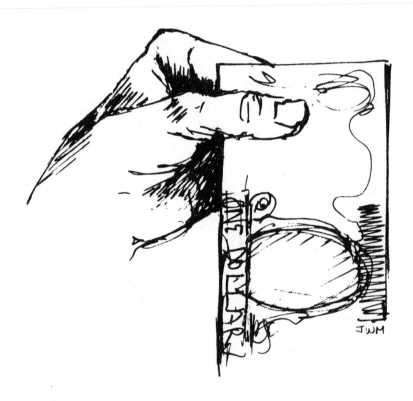

Hold a dollar bill by one corner in your left hand. Let the rest of the bill dangle. Spread the thumb and forefinger of your right hand so that the fingers encircle the bill down at the bottom of the bill. Release bill from your left hand and show how easy it is to catch the bill between the thumb and fore-

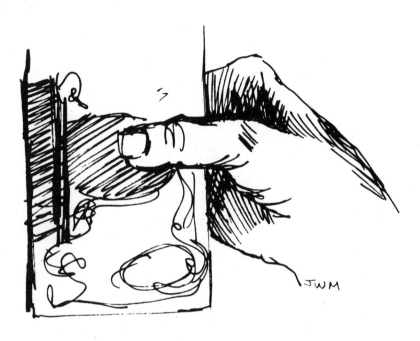

finger. Catch the bill so that your thumb lands on Washington's picture.

Now bet that they can't catch the bill while you drop it. Hold the corner of the bill, and tell the bettor to encircle the bill with his thumb and forefinger and try to catch the bill with the two fingers only. It's almost impossible to catch, if they don't cheat!

GRANDMA'S DOORMAT

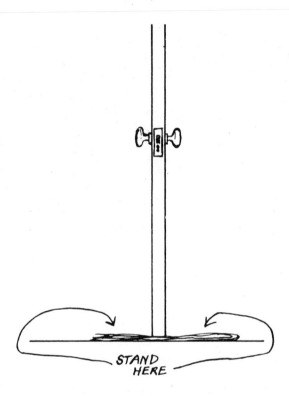

STAND
HERE

Bet someone that it's possible to place newspaper on the floor in such a way that two persons can stand on it together and yet not be able to touch each other.

The secret is to place the paper on the floor in a doorway and then close the door over it, with one person on each side of the door.

A QUICKIE!

Bet someone that he cannot pour a glass of liquid down his neck without getting wet. The solution . . . drink it!

THE PAPER ROPE

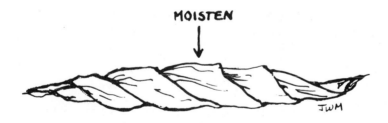

MOISTEN

JWM

Twist a paper napkin into a rope and invite anyone to break it with a steady pull. It is almost impossible!

That is, unless you first secretly moisten it near the center.

TIME OUT

Bet your friends that they cannot remember whether the number "6" on their watches is printed in Roman (VI) or Arabic (6) numerals.

The answer is that in many watches, the second hand occupies the 6 space! Naturally, it won't work with a watch with a "sweep second" hand.

INTO THE BOTTLE

Place a bottle on the floor inside a door and bet that you can crawl into it.

The demonstration looks silly, but get into the other room with the bottle opening facing toward you, and crawl *in to* it.

CIGARETTE BREAK

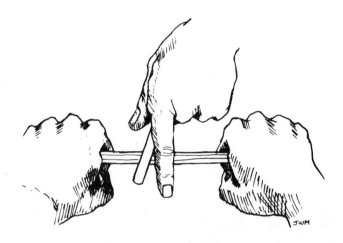

Have a friend hold the ends of a pencil between his two hands tightly, leaving about three inches of pencil showing. Hold a cigarette extended from your clenched fist, and bet that you can break the pencil with the cigarette.

With a quick "down-sweep," secretly extend your forefinger, breaking the pencil. Apparently the cigarette broke it!

WRITER'S CRAMP

Bet someone that you will tell him something he cannot write. Have him write, in numerals, the number eleven thousand, eleven hundred and eleven. The answer is 12,111.

Then ask him to write, "There are three 2's in the English language." There is no *correct* way to write the sentence or to spell (to, two, too), tuse or tuze!

COCKTAIL MIX

Bet your buddy that you can pour water on top of soda or liquor without mixing them—and then drink the drink and leave the water.

First, float a small piece of paper on the drink. Then carefully, with a spoon, put a film of water over this. You have poured water without mixing! To get the liquor or soda out, drink it from a straw.

STOOD UP

Bet that you can make someone come down from a chair by merely commanding "Get down!" (He has to come down sometime).

HOT FORK GAG

Place three forks on a table edge. Bet one of your guests that he cannot pick up the center one without using his hands.

Most people will use their teeth, so coat the underside of the center fork handle with hot mustard.

DIME DOWNFALL

Break a wooden match halfway through, but don't break it entirely. Form a V-shape and place the match on top of a small whiskey glass and put a dime on top of it.

Now bet that without touching the coin or the match, you can make the dime fall into the glass.

The secret is to drop some water on the split center of the match. The wood fibers will expand, and the dime will drop in!

COIN IN GLASS

INSIDE OF HAT

Balance a man's hat (or an open tin can) on its side, upon a glass. Then, carefully balance a coin on top of the hat (or can) directly above the glass. Give the hat a sharp blow and the hat will fly leaving the coin in the glass.

The secret is to give a very sharp quick blow *inside* the hat brim. Bet the bystanders to repeat your act! We bet they can't.

ANOTHER COIN DROP

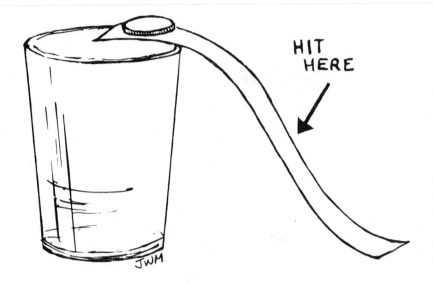

HIT
HERE

Lay a heavy strip of paper on the edge of a glass.
Balance a coin on the paper and edge of the glass.
    When all bets are covered, strike a sharp down-
ward blow at the midpoint and the coin will fall
into the glass.

HEAVY!

Place an apple and an orange (or any two objects,
for that matter) in front of your friend. Bet him that

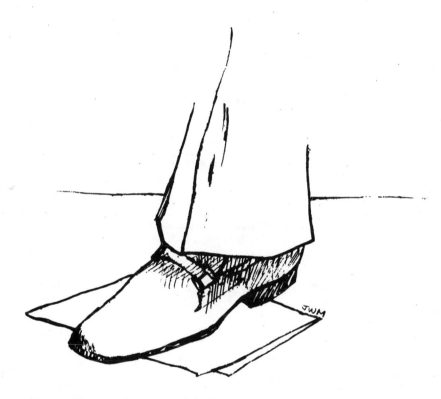

he cannot lift either of them alone.

You win—no matter which he lifts, you say, "You are not alone, I'm here!"

THE MINDREADER

Ask someone to write a message on a piece of paper, fold it, and stand on it. Then bet that you can tell him *what is on it*. The answer is "You are!"

A HOT ONE

Place a piece of paper on top of a glass. Now place a dime on top of the paper directly over the glass.

Bet that you can make the dime fall into the glass without touching the paper, glass or coin.

Ignite the paper with a match!

SUPERFINGERS

Have a woman place her hands firmly against her chest with the finger tips just touching. Bet someone that they cannot pull the hands apart. If the girl's wrists are grasped firmly, an attempt to pull the hands apart is close to impossible.

Do not stand sideways or attempt to jerk the

hands, but exert a steady pull, at arm's length or with both arms bent to improve the leverage.

STRONG ARM

Bet someone that he cannot hold an ordinary book straight at arm's length, at shoulder height, for ten minutes. Impossible to do!

ANOTHER HOT ONE

Bet that you can set fire to a handkerchief without injuring it.

Dip part of a handkerchief in brandy, then set a

light to it. The flame will spread all over it. When the alcohol is consumed, the moist part that remains will put the fire out.

THE MAGNETIZED GLASS

Bet your host that you can magnetize a glass. A glass with a hollow bottom is required. The bottom rim is slightly dampened before the stunt is performed. Press the palm down firmly upon the bottom and the slight vacuum formed will be strong enough to support the weight of the glass.

HEADS I WIN

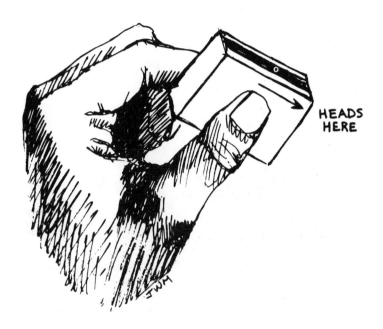

HEADS HERE

Bet your buddy that you can tell which direction the heads of the matches in a box of safety matches are pointing without looking inside the box.

Shake the box and win every time since you can feel that the head ends are heavier than the tails by grasping the box very lightly in the center. The added weight of the head ends will lower one end of the box. Try it once or twice and you will even *hear* the difference!

P.S.: Use a full box.

TOSSING FOR DRINKS

BOX FALLS
WITH COIN DOWN

COIN
BETWEEN
DRAWER
AND
COVER

A box of safety matches thrown into the air will land on the table label-side up every time (well, almost every time), if you secretly place a heavy coin in the bottom of the box between the drawer and the case. The weight of the coin causes the bottom of the box to fall downward.

Permit your barmate to toss first, and tell him you will pay for the drinks if you cannot match his toss. Naturally, you will win almost every toss.

THROUGH THE TUNNEL

Break open the cover of a match box and set it so that it forms a tunnel. Place the empty box drawer on the side of the cover opposite you.

Bet anyone to bring the drawer through the tunnel without touching it!

Here's how. Cup your hand in back of the drawer. Blow hard against the palm of your hand. The air will reflect and force the drawer through the tunnel.

TWO CENTS PLAIN

Balance two coins on the edge of a glass. Challenge someone to remove them both at the same time, using only the thumb and one finger of the same hand.

Grip the coins with the tips of the thumb and middle finger of one hand, causing them to slide down the side of the glass. Then draw them around the side of the glass and snap them together.

BOTTOMS UP

Lay a coin on the bottom of an inverted tumbler.

Bet that it is impossible to lift the coin "from the top of the glass" with two matches.

Let them try it and lose. They did not lift the coin "from the *top* of the glass," but the bottom!

1000

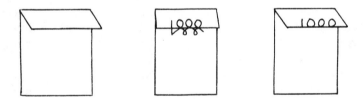

Bet that you can write the number 1000 without lifting the pencil from the paper.

To do it, fold the edge of the paper down. Then trace the figure seen in Picture 1. When you lift the pencil, the number 1000 will appear on the bottom of the sheet.

THE ARCHITECT'S PUZZLE

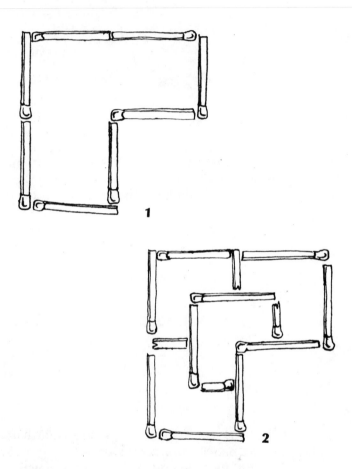

An architect's problem is to divide a lot equally. Let's help him! Arrange eight matches to form the figure in Picture 1. Hand your buddy four extra matches, and challenge him to *divide the area of the figure into four equal areas, each the same size and shape!*

His four matches may be broken in any way, but the original eight matches must not be moved.

See Picture 2 for the answer. Two of the matches are broken in half to do the job!

THE SECRET

1

Using twelve matches, form Picture 1.

Now ask someone to rearrange the position of only two matches, and reveal the secret of *"what makes the world go round."*

The answer is "LOVE" (see picture 2)! LOVE is *really* the answer!

5 + 6 = 9

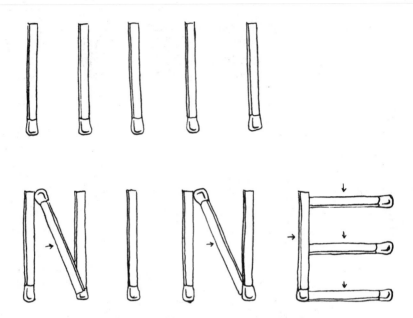

Challenge your friends to add 5 to 6 and make 9. Here's how. Lay five matches on the table, add the other six matches to spell out the word *NINE!*

THE SIX GLASSES

Three empty glasses and three filled glasses are required. Arrange the glasses from left to right: 1) empty, 2) empty, 3) full, 4) full, 5) full, 6) empty. Now, challenge someone to arrange the glasses

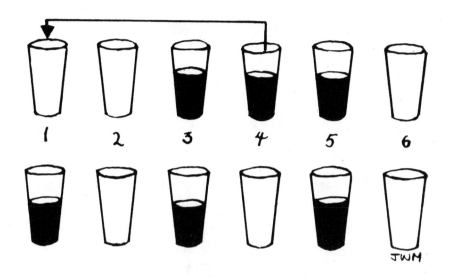

so they stand alternately one filled, one empty, one filled, one empty, one filled, one empty. *This must be done by touching or moving only one glass!*

Secret: Lift glass #4 and pour contents into glass #1. Replace #4 in its original spot.

THE FLYING MATCH

Place three matches as shown in the sketch, two of them thrust in between the drawer and the sides of the box. Light the cross match in the middle and bet which end will ignite first.

After all the opinions and bets are in, light the

central match and watch the fun. The pressure of the other two matches will throw the burning stick in the air. The others do not light.

You win every time, since their bets never are correct.

BRIDGE OF KNIVES

Using three glasses as bases, bet that you can form

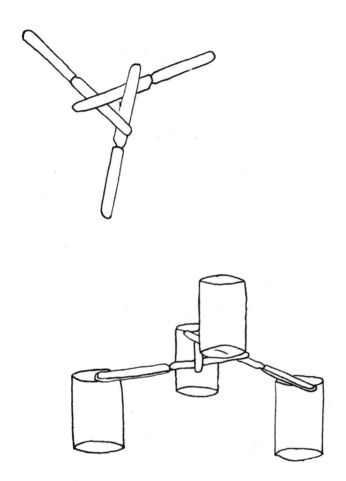

a three-way bridge, with three knives, each knife using a glass as its base.

The blades of the knives, are interlocked, and the handles rest on the glasses.

KNOTS TO YOU

Bet someone that you can tie in a knot in a hand-kerchief or a length of cord without letting go of the ends.

The secret: Fold your arms, grasp the ends of the handkerchief and unfold the arms without letting go of the ends. A knot will appear if done correctly.

SMOKE DREAM

Bet that you can cause a cigarette to smoke itself. Hold a lighted cigarette as shown, squeeze the

palms together and relax them. Repeat again and again.

THE STRIPPER

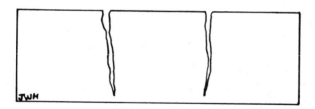

A three-inch strip of narrow paper is torn almost all of the way through in two places, each about an inch away from the other.

Bet anyone to completely tear the paper strip so

that the center piece will fall free. You win every time!

No matter how they pull, the center piece will always stay fastened to one of the end pieces!

UNDER WATER

Here's a "swindle" which will keep them guessing until you tell the secret. Bet that *you can light a match under water!*

Have a glass of water held up high in the air, and merely light the match (under the water).

Now step back before the water is poured on your head!

TWO STRAIGHT ROWS

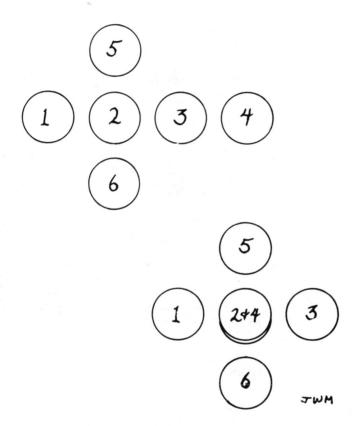

JWM

Arrange six coins, as in picture 1. Bet everyone that they cannot arrange the six coins, so that they form two straight rows of four coins each.

The secret is sort of a swindle. Place coin 4 on top of coin 2.

THE ACROBATIC FLAME

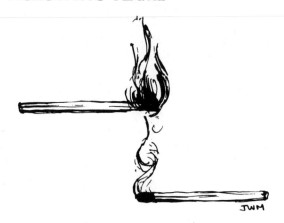

Bet your friends that you can make a match light by remote control.

Light two matches, blow one out and as the smoke rises hold the flame of the other match above it. The flame will slide down the curl of smoke and relight the lower match without direct contact.

Blow out the match again and repeat the relighting in "instant replay."

VANISHING SQUARES

Arrange twenty matchsticks to form seven squares (see picture 1). Bet that you can make two squares vanish, leaving only five squares, the same size as the original seven. *Only three matches may be moved!*

The way to do it is to remove three matches as in picture 2 and replace them as in picture 3.

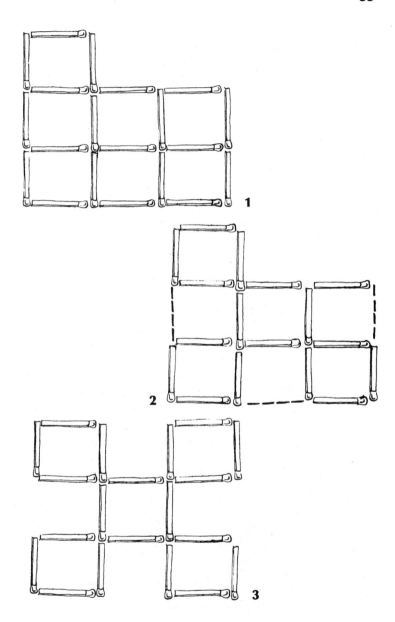

1

2

3

THE HOUDINI DIME

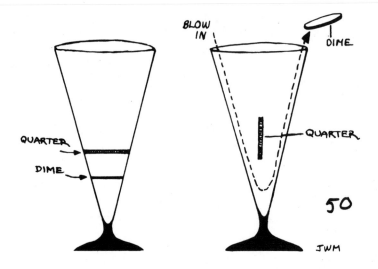

Set a dime in a tapered glass. Drop a quarter on top of the dime to entrap the dime within the glass.

Bet anyone to remove the dime without touching the quarter. Here's how: Blow down one side of the tumbler, causing the quarter to tilt over edgewise and the dime to slide out of the glass.

TOUCHDOWN

1) Can you place four golf balls so that each ball touches the other three?
2) Can you arrange five coins so that each coin touches the other four?
3) Can you arrange seven cigarettes so that each cigarette touches the other six?

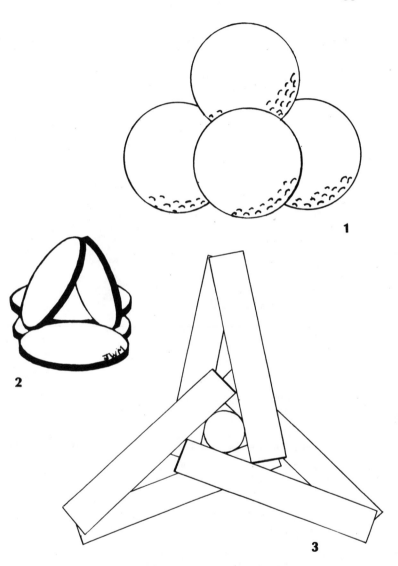

To win all three bets, place them as in the pictures.

THE MAGNETIC CIGAR

Bet that you can magnetize a cigar, and demonstrate by causing it to adhere to your fingertip.

Push a bent pin through the cigar band. The point of the pin rests on the fingertip. Throw away the pin and let them try it.

Henny Youngman's
Bar Jokes

BAR JOKES

Two Jewish mothers talking—one says to the other,
"I haven't seen you in a long time—how is your son,
and what is he doing?"

She says, "My son is a famous doctor in California
and he's making a fortune. He just built a new
home that cost $300,000." She says to the other
woman, "What is your son doing?"

She says, "My son is doing fine—he's a homo-
sexual and he lives in Hollywood. He just moved in
with a doctor who has a $300,000 home."

A cop stops a guy who has been speeding. He says
to the guy, "What are you speeding so fast for?"

The guy says, "I'm sick."

The cop looks in the car and sees a racing form
on the seat. "I see you have a racing form, and
you're probably speeding to the track, and you say
you're sick."

The guy says, "Oh, is that a sickness!"

59

There was a show in New York called "Oh Calcutta," where everybody on stage was naked. I wouldn't go to see that.

I went home, I looked in the mirror, I saved $12.00!

A hold-up man goes into the bank—he sticks a gun in the cashier's face, and says, "Give me all your cash."

The cashier says, "Here, take the books too, I'm $10,000 bucks short."

A traveling salesman on the road stops off at a little restaurant. He orders two eggs.

They only have one egg left, so the waitress says to the chef, "Throw anything you have in the kitchen into it, he won't know the difference."

So the chef throws in a piece of old limburger cheese with the egg.

The man has his breakfast, and calls the waitress over. He says to the waitress, "Where do you get your eggs?"

She says, "We have our own chickens."

He says, "Do you have a rooster?"

She says, "No."

He says, "You better get one, because there's a skunk been fooling around with one of your chickens."

I discovered a new blood control device. My wife takes off her make-up.

———————

A panhandler walks up to a man. He says, "Would you mind helping a man out of work? All I have in this whole world is this gun!"

———————

One fellow says to another, "Who was that lady I saw you with last night?"
"That was no lady, that was my brother-in-law. We're just sick about it!"

———————

Linda Lovelace, star of "Deep Throat," says she's not going to make any more X-rated pictures.
She's had it up to here!

———————

Elevator stops on the third floor and a nude woman walks into the elevator.
The guy in the elevator doesn't know what to say—he finally says, "My wife has an outfit just like yours."

———————

A fellow goes to Confession—"Father, my wife and I took a vow we wouldn't have sex during Lent, and we broke our vow."

The Priest said, "What happened?"

"She was leaning over a potato sack, and she looked so cute, and as we're newlyweds, I couldn't help myself, and we made love there and then."

"What happened?"

"They threw us out of the A&P!"

A guy says to a Rabbi, "You have such a small congregation. How much do you make a week?"

The Rabbi says, "Six dollars a week."

He says, "How can you live on that?"

"If I wasn't a very religious man, and didn't fast three days a week, I'd starve to death!"

A mother says to her son, "Get out of bed and go to school."

He says, "I don't want to go to school."

She says, "Eight o'clock in the morning, you go to school."

"I don't want to go to school—the kids don't like me, the janitor don't like me, and the teachers don't like me."

"You're forty-five years old, and you're the principal. Go to school!"

A woman says to her husband, "Suppose you came home one night and found another man making love to me, what would you do?"

He says, "I'd kick his seeing-eye dog!"

A man walks into his doctor's office and says, "Doctor, I have sex only once a week."

Doctor says, "How old are you?"

He says, "Seventy-three."

Doctor says, "You're seventy-three, and have sex once a week. I think that's wonderful. What are you complaining about?"

"My neighbor is seventy-six years old, and he says he has sex six times a week."

The doctor says, "You say the same thing!"

A young woman goes to a doctor.

The doctor says, "Get undressed."

She says, "Turn out the lights."

He says, "After all, I'm a doctor."

She says, "Turn out the lights."

So the doctor turns out the lights.

Five minutes later, she says, "Where shall I put my clothes?"

He says, "On top of mine!"

In Israel on top of a hill is the Israeli Guard.

On the other side is the Arab Guard.

The Israeli Guard is shouting out, "Thirteen, thirteen, thirteen."

The annoyed Arab Guard shouts out to him—"What are you hollering out thirteen all the time for? What does that mean?"

The Israeli Guard says, "Come over here, I'll show you." He says to the Arab Guard, "Look over that cliff."

He kicks the Arab over the cliff. He starts hollering out, "Fourteen, fourteen, fourteen!"

A fellow from New York joins the Israeli Army. He is in the army three days, and asks for a three-day leave of absence.

The Colonel says, "What are you, a nut from New York? You are in the army three days, you ask for a three-day pass?" To get a three-day pass, you have to do something sensational."

The next day, the guy comes back driving an Arab tank all by himself.

The amazed Colonel says, "How did you do it?"

He says, "I took one of our tanks and went towards Jordan. I saw one of their tanks coming towards me. The Arab put up a white flag, I put up a white flag. I said to him, 'Do you want to get a three-day pass?' He says 'Yes,' so we exchanged tanks."

A guy has a dream that God told him to have himself fixed up. So the guy has a hair transplant, he gets a nose job, he reduces and becomes nice and slim, buys new clothes. All of a sudden, he is struck by lightning, and winds up in heaven.

He gets to heaven, and God doesn't even talk to him.

He shouts at God, "You told me in my dreams to better myself. I had a nose job, I had a hair transplant, I took off weight—now you don't even talk to me."

God says, "Don't holler at me, I didn't even recognize you, Irving."

My wife wanted her face lifted. They couldn't do that, but for $80.00 they lowered her body.

Sam got a dollar too much in his pay envelope and said nothing about it, but the following week the paymaster discovered his error, so he deducted a dollar from Sam's pay.

Sam put up a big squawk, so the paymaster said, "Funny you didn't complain last week when you were a dollar over," and Sam said, "That's right, because a guy can overlook one mistake but when it happens twice, it's time to complain!"

A couple of cloak-and-suiters were discussing their problems in the garment district, when one of them said, "You know that Liebowitz, he's fooling around with his models." The other said, "So what? Everybody down here does that, even I do it," and his friend said, "Yeah, but Liebowitz is in MEN'S CLOTHING!"

While playing golf today, I hit two good balls. I stepped on a rake!

The guy was talking to his friend, and said, "My wife is in the next room and is about to have a baby."

His friend said, "Where's the doctor?"

He said, "I don't need the doctor, I deliver the baby myself."

All of a sudden, a scream from the next room.

He rushes in. Five minutes later, he comes out, "It's a boy!" All of a sudden, another scream, he rushes in, comes out five minutes later, says, "It's twins this time." Another scream—he rushes in—he comes out, and says, "This time its triplets!" Now, one more scream—he rushes out the front door.

His friend says, "Where are you going?"

"I want to find out how you shut the damn thing off."

A woman called another woman on the phone and asked her how she was feeling. The other woman said, "Terrible! My head's splitting and my back and legs are killing me and the house is a mess and the children are simply driving me crazy."

The caller said, "Lissen, go and lie down, I'll come right over and cook lunch for you and you get some rest. By the way, how's your husband, Sam?"

The woman said, "Sam? I got no husband, Sam."

The first woman said, "My goodness, I must have dialed the wrong number."

The complaining woman said, "Then you're not coming over?"

A 70-year-old man married a girl of 20, and immediately was given advice by his friends. One of them said, "If you want a happy marriage, you must take in a boarder." This appealed to the old man, and a few months later he met his friend who wanted to know how things were coming along.

The old man said, "Things couldn't be better, and I owe it all to your good advice."

His friend said, "I'm glad to hear it, and how's your wife?"

The old guy said, "Oh, she's pregnant."

His friend said, "That's great, and the boarder?" and the old man said, "Oh, she's pregnant, too!"

"I understand your husband got drowned and left you two million dollars. Can you imagine, two million dollars, and he couldn't even read or write."

She said, "Yeah . . . and he couldn't swim either."

A guy walks into the Stage Delicatessen, orders barley and bean soup. The waiter says, *Nemnisht*, which in Jewish means, *don't take it*.

The man walks over to the boss and says, "Where did you get the Chinese waiter who speaks Jewish?"

"Don't say anything, he thinks I'm teaching him English."

A little Jewish man died in a town. He must have been a horrible man because no one wanted to say a good word at his funeral. Not even the local Rabbi. So they asked a Rabbi in the next town.

He said, "I didn't like him either, but I'll say a few good words."

He gets up at the funeral and says, "His brother was worse!"

At our country club, one of the members dropped dead. Nobody wanted to tell his wife, so the doctor said he'd do it.

He called, and said, "Mrs. Cohen, your husband Sam lost $500 playing cards at the club."

The wife yelled, "He should drop dead."

The doctor said, "He did."

This Irish guy drops dead. Who should tell the wife—and how? A guy volunteers. He knocks on the door—a lady comes out—he says, "Is this the Widow Ryan?"

"I'm not the Widow Ryan."

"Wait until you see what they're dragging in the back door."

I knew a woman who went to an HMO, where they had about eight doctors. After 15 minutes in one doctor's office, she ran screaming down the hall. Another doctor, who finally got the story out of her, called the first doctor. "What's the idea of telling Miss Jones she's pregnant? She isn't. You frightened her to death."

"I know," the first doctor said, "but I cured her hiccups, didn't I?"

A salesman was trying to sell a bachelor a new car, and pointing to the dashboard, he said, "See this panel? All buttons! You press the red one and a redhead gets in the car with you. If you press the black button, a brunette gets in! If you press this yellow button, a beautiful blonde gets in the car."

The bachelor said, "Gee, that's great."

The salesman said, "Well, do you want the car?" and the bachelor said, "No. just sell me the buttons!"

Three scientists were given six months to live and they were told they could have anything they wanted. The first scientist was a Frenchman, and he wanted a beautiful villa on the Riviera, surrounded by gorgeous young girls. The second scientist was an Englishman, and he wanted to have tea with the Queen. The third was a Jewish scientist. He wanted the opinion of another doctor!

A movie producer advertised for a Texan, 6 feet tall, weighing 200 lbs. One morning, about 3 o'clock, he got a phone call in answer to the ad from a fellow who spoke with a Jewish accent.

The producer said, "You don't sound like a Texan," and the fellow said, "That's right, I ain't, I'm from New York."

The producer said, "Are you 6 feet tall and do you weigh 200 lbs.?" and the fellow said, "No, I'm five feet-five and I weigh 110 lbs."

The producer was furious as he yelled, "Then what the hell are you phoning me for at 3 o'clock in the morning?" and the Jewish feller said, "I just called to tell you, ON ME YOU SHOULDN'T DEPEND!"

A traveling man went on the road for a month, but kept staying away. Every few weeks he'd send his wife a wire, saying, "Can't come home, still buying!" Every wire was the same, "Can't come home, still buying." This went on for three or four months, when his wife finally sent him a wire that said, "Better come home, I'm selling what you're buying!"

An elderly man approaches a prostitute. "How about a little fun?"

She says, "How old are you?"

He says, "Eighty."

She says, "You've already had it."

He says, "How much do I owe you?"

A minister gave a talk to the Lion's Club on sex. When he got home he couldn't tell his wife that he talked about sex, so he told her he spoke about yachting and boating.

A few weeks later, she ran into some people in the village and they complimented her on the speech her husband made.

She said, "Yes, I heard. I was surprised about the subject matter as he had only tried it twice. First time he got sick, and the second time his hat blew off."

A guy asked another man, "What do you think of this Watergate scandal?"

The other man, who stuttered, said, "They oughta

oughta oughta take take take all all all those guys and throw throw throw them out of the government, and start start anew."

The other guy said, "That's easy for you to say."

A guy has a new pet, a little pussy cat, and he falls in love with the little pussy cat. The pussy cat follows him around, and he is just crazy about the pussy cat. The man wins a free trip to Paris and he leaves the pussy cat with his brother.

Two weeks later, he calls his brother from Paris. He says over the phone, "How is my little pussy cat?"

The brother says, "Your pussy cat died."

He says, "Why did you have to tell it to me that way for? You could have told me the pussy cat was on the roof, he broke his leg, and I would have gotten used to it, gradually."

The brother says, "Forgive me, I'm sorry."

"O.K., I forgive you. By the way, how is Mom?"

"She's on the roof."

A guy goes to court for a divorce. The Judge says, "Why do you want a divorce?"

He says, "Every night, when I come home from work, instead of my wife being alone, I find a different guy hiding in the closet."

The Judge says, "And this causes you a lot of unhappiness."

The man said, "It certainly does, Judge, I never have any room to hang up my clothes."

Girl fell overboard. Father said, "I'll give half my fortune to save her."

Fellow jumps in—saves girl.

"I'll keep my promise—here's half my fortune."

"I don't want money, all I want to know is who shoved me."

A rich old garment manufacturer died and his family met in the lawyer's office for the reading of his will.

He left $300,000 to his wife, $100,000 to his brothers, and $10,000 each to his sisters.

Then the will read: "And to my nephew Irving, who always wanted to be mentioned in my will, I say, 'Hello, Irving!' "

A man goes down to a ship company. He wants to know the cheapest trip he can get to Bermuda.

The clerk says, "We can give you a suite for $2,500."

"No, that's too expensive."

"Well, we have a room for $500."

He says, "That's too expensive, what is the cheapest trip you have?"

"We have one trip where you get in a boat with 12 guys and you row across!"

A stockbroker catches his wife in bed with another man.

He says to her, "What's going on here."
"Believe it or not, John, I've gone public!"

A couple celebrating their fiftieth wedding anniversary—they go down to their old school—there, in a corner, was their old desk where he had carved on the desk, "I love you, Sadie," and he remembered where he had put her hair in the inkwell.

On the way home, a Federal Reserve truck's back door opens and money drops out. She picks up the money and counts it—$50,000.

The husband says, "Give the money back!"

She says, "No, finders keepers."

When they get home, she hides the money in the attic.

The next day, two FBI men show up at their home.

They say, "Pardon me, did any one in this house find any money that fell out of a Federal Reserve truck yesterday?"

She says, "No."

The husband says, "My wife's lying, she found the money and put it up in the attic."

She says, "Don't believe him, he's a little senile."

So they sit the man down and question him.

The FBI man says, "Tell us the story from the beginning."

The man says, "My wife and I were coming home from school."

The FBI man says, "Let's get the hell out of here!"

A holdup man holds up a woman.

She says, "I haven't got any money."

He says, "I'll feel around your body, and see if you're telling the truth."

Finally, he says, "Go ahead."

She says, "Don't stop now, I'll write a check."

A dentist has been having a romance with one of his patients.

She is sitting in the dentist's chair, and he says, "Darling, we can't see each other any more, you're down to your last tooth."

A man goes to a psychiatrist—the psychiatrist says to the man, "What do you do for a living?"

He says, "I'm an auto mechanic."

The psychiatrist says, "Get under the couch."

A man has been smoking cigarettes for 20 years. He takes one puff from a cigarette, throws it down and steps on it.

He does this all day long. What do you think this man has today?

Cancer of the shoe.

Two guys in a gym—one guy is putting a girdle on.

His friend says, "Since when are you wearing a girdle?"

"Since my wife found it in the glove compartment of my car."

A guy says to another guy, "How many times have you been married?"

He says, "Twice."

"What happened to your first wife?"

He says, "She fell in the wishing well."

I didn't know they worked!

A panhandler asks me for a dollar for a cup of coffee.

I start to follow him.

He said, "What are you following me for?"

"I want to be sure you don't buy a bowl of soup!"

Two furriers were returning from Miami, and just for the kick of it decided to take a taxi back to New York.

As they were climbing in the cab, one of them said, "Let me get in the cab first, I'm getting out at 72nd Street."

A cross-eyed judge was trying three cross-eyed prisoners.

He turned to the first cross-eyed prisoner, and said, "What's your name?"

And the second cross-eyed prisoner said, "John Brown," and the cross-eyed judge said, "I wasn't talking to you," and the third cross-eyed prisoner said, "I didn't say anything."

Two fellows applying for a job as truck drivers.

One says, "This is my partner, Sam. My name is Orville."

"O.K., Orville, I want to give you a mental test. Suppose you are driving along a road at 3 o'clock in the morning, and you are on a little bridge, and another truck is coming towards you at 100 miles an hour, what is the first thing you'd do?"

"I'd wake up my partner, Sam, and say this is the greatest wreck you'll ever see."

———

Two Israelis are about to be shot by six Arabs.

One Israeli says to the other one, "I think I'm going to ask for a blindfold."

The other says, "Sam, don't make trouble."

———

A man brags about his new hearing-aid. "It's the most expensive I've ever had—it cost $2,500."

His friend asks, "What kind is it?"

He says, "Half-past-four!"

———

A woman who never gets taken anywhere by her husband.

She says, "What would it take for you to go on a second honeymoon?"

He says, "A second wife!"

Three women at a Hadassah dinner. One says, "My husband bought me an estate in Mt. Kisco, New York."

The other woman says, "I have a beautiful home up in Rye."

The third woman, who lives in the Bronx, says, "I live three stations from Scarsdale!"

A couple go to a doctor and complain that they are having trouble with their sex life, what can they do about it?

The doctor says, "The trouble with you people is that you don't communicate with each other. Make believe that you are making love on a yacht."

They get home that night, and as they are making love, he says to her, "Make believe we're out on a yacht out on the ocean." After a minute, he says to her, "Are you sailing yet?"

She says, "No."

A minute later, he says to her, "Are you sailing yet?"

She says, "No."

Another minute goes by, and he says, "Are you sailing yet?"

She says, "No."

He says, "Bon Voyage."

This guy dies and leaves the shortest will. It said, "Being in my sound mind, I spent my money!"

There is a man stretched out on his back on four seats in the theatre—the usher comes down, and says to him, "Mister, you will have to get out of those four seats; you are only entitled to one seat."

The man grunts, and doesn't move.

The manager of the theatre walks down. He says to the man who is still lying on the four seats, "Mister, you'll have to get out of there, all you're entitled to is one seat."

The man grunts, and doesn't move.

Now the policeman comes down. The policeman says, "Get out of those seats."

The man grunts.

The policeman says, "O.K. wise guy, where are you from?"

"The balcony!"

A little Jewish man gets on the bus—he sees a friend on the bus—he says to him, "You couldn't get a cab either!"

Two guys meet. One says, "You look bad, what's the matter with you?"

He says, "I was in London where there was a six-hour difference in time, and I couldn't sleep, and my timing is off. I sit down to eat, I get sleepy, I go to bed, I get hungry."

A Lufthansa airplane goes down and lands on the ocean ten miles from Germany.

The captain shouts over a microphone, "All those who can swim, get on top of the right wing. All those who can't swim, get on top of the left wing.

"You people who can swim, start swimming—you are only ten miles to shore.

"All those who can't swim—thank you for flying Lufthansa."

A man was taking a survey on the vaseline industry. He knocks on the lady's door. He says, "I represent a vaseline company and we are taking a survey of the many uses of vaseline in the home. Do you happen to use vaseline in your home, Madame?"

She says, "Yes."

He says, "How many ways do you use it?"

She says, "We use it for cuts, bruises and sex."

He says, "How do you use it for sex?"

She says, "We put it on the door-knob—it keeps the kids out of the room."

Vasectomy means never having to say you're sorry!

A fellow walked up to a tourist in New York and said, "Do you know where Central Park is?"

The tourist said, "No."

He said, "O.K., so I'll mug you here!"

A middle-aged lady goes to a doctor.

He says, "Get undressed . . . Lady, that's the ugliest body I've ever seen."

She says, "That's what my doctor told me."

"What did you come to me for?"

"I wanted another doctor's opinion!"

———

We've been married 45 years . . . went back to the same hotel where we got married . . . had the same suite of rooms . . . only this time *I* went in the bathroom and cried.

———

This prisoner is going to the electric chair.

The warden says, "You can have anything you want for your last meal."

The prisoner says, "I want strawberries."

The warden says, "Strawberries won't be in season for six months."

The prisoner says, "I'll wait."

———

I got a great lawyer. He had the charge of sodomy changed to walking too close.

———

Two Jewish women in the building—one says to the

other, "Did you hear there is a rapist in the building?"

She says, "Yes I know, I already gave!"

Two guys at a bar, one says, "I don't know what's
wrong with my wife, every time we make love she
blacks out on me."

His friend says, "Yeah, how about that?"

A guy owns a delicatessen. Two Internal Revenue
men come to see him.

The delicatessen guy says, "I slave all day to
make a living for my wife and family, and you question my measly $6,000 a year income."

The tax guy says, "It's not your income we question, it's the six trips to Israel that you and your
family made last year."

He says, "Oh that, I forgot to tell you we also
deliver."

A couple check into a hotel right next to a railroad
station. The only room left in town.

The man goes out to take a walk, the woman lies
down to take a rest. All of a sudden, a train goes by
at about 100 miles an hour and the vibration from
the train knocks the woman out of bed.

Ten minutes, another train comes by so close that the vibrations knock her out of bed again.

She calls down and complains to the manager. She says, "What kind of a hotel is this? A train came by so close that the vibration of the train knocked me out of bed twice."

The manager sarcastically says, "I'd like to see that!"

She says, "Come on upstairs." He comes up. She says, "Lay down in that bed for a minute." He lays down.

Just then her husband walks in. "What are you doing in that bed?"

He says, "Believe it or not, I'm waiting for a train."

A Jewish woman had two chickens as pets. One chicken got sick, so she killed the other one to make chicken soup for the sick one.

A drunk walked up to a parking meter and put in a dime. The dial went to 60. He said, "How about that. I lost 100 pounds."

Two drunks walking along Broadway in New York. One goes down into the subway by mistake. Comes up the other entrance and his friend is waiting for him.

The waiting drunk says, "Where were you?"

The other one says, "I was in some guy's basement. Has he got a set of trains!"

Want to drive somebody crazy? Send him a wire saying, "Ignore first wire."

In Hollywood they have community property. A couple gets divorced, she gets the Jaguar, he gets the little cap.

A man and a woman in a room. All of a sudden, a knock on the door.
  She says, "Quick, hide, that's my husband."
  He says, "Where's the back door?"
  She says, "We haven't got one."
  He says, "Where would you like one?"

Two newlyweds—he's 64 and she's 23. She catches him cheating with a 48-year-old woman.
  She says, "What has she got I haven't got?"
  He says, "Patience!"

An elderly couple go to a doctor. The man says, "We want to know if we're making love properly. Will you look at us?"

The doctor says, "Go ahead." So they make love.

The doctor says, "You're making love perfectly. That will be $10.00."

They come back six weeks in a row, and do the same thing.

The seventh visit, the doctor said, "What are you coming here like this for—I told you you're making love properly."

The man says, "She can't come to my house, I can't go to her house. You charge us $10.00, the motel costs us $20.00, and we get $8.00 back from Medicaire.

All you married men, want to drive your wives crazy? When you go home, don't talk in your sleep— just *grin*.

They have a new thing nowadays called Nicotine Anonymous. It's for people who want to stop smoking. When you feel a craving for a cigarette, you simply call up another member and he comes over and you get drunk together.

The two biggest features on the new cars are air-brakes and unbreakable windshields. You can speed up to one hundred miles an hour and stop on a dime. Then you press a special button and a putty knife scrapes you off the windshield.

A little old lady walked up to a cop and said, "I was attacked—I was attacked!"

He said, "When?"

She said, "Twenty years ago."

He said, "What are you telling me now for?"

She said, "I like to talk about it once in a while."

A woman called up the police department and said, "I have a sex maniac in my apartment. Pick him up in the morning."

If you must drink while you're driving home, be sure the radio in the car is turned up loud. That way you won't hear the crash.

Two drunks were standing in front of the Washington monument. One of them started a fire at the base of it. The other said, "You'll never get it off the ground."

He said, "I love you terribly." She said, "You certainly do."

Americans are getting stronger. Twenty years ago it took two people to carry ten dollars' worth of groceries. Today a five-year-old does it.

In her own eyes, Peggy was the most popular girl in the world. "You know," she said, with characteristic modesty, "A lot of men are going to be miserable when I marry."

"Really?" said her date, stifling a yawn. "How many are you going to marry?"

A doctor gave a guy six months to live, and he didn't pay his bill. So the doctor gave him six more months to live.

A traveling salesman's car broke down on a lonely country road one night. It was storming but the salesman could see a farmhouse light not too far away. He made his way to the door and the farmer, being a friendly guy, invited the salesman in to have something to eat.

The farmer's beautiful young wife served a delicious meal and offered the salesman some homemade cottage cheese. The salesman having fully enjoyed the meal, replied that he would prefer putting it in the refrigerator for later.

The salesman asked the farmer if he could put him up for the night. The farmer apologized. The only place he had was in bed with him and his wife, but it was a large bed and there would be room if the salesman didn't mind. The salesman was delighted and graciously accepted.

As fate would have it, in the middle of the night the farmer had to get out of bed to tend a cow who chose that inopportune time to deliver her calf.

When the farmer had gone out to the barn, the farmer's lovely, alluring wife leaned over and whispered in the salesman's ear that now was his chance.

The salesman slyly smiled, and agreed. Whereupon, he jumped out of bed, raced to the kitchen, tore open the refrigerator, grabbed the cottage cheese, and ate it.

A doctor asked his woman patient, "Do you know what the most effective birth control pill is?"

She replied, "No."

He said, "That's it!"

An English flyer was shot down over Russia during the Second World War and wound up in a Russian hospital.

The doctor fixed him up but told him he would have to amputate his right leg to save his life.

After the flyer recovered from the shock of the bad news, he asked the doctor if he would do him one favor.

The doctor being a compassionate man said that he would try.

The flyer said, "Would you give the leg to one of your flyers and have him drop it over England. Hip, Hip."

The doctor agreed, and it was done.

A week later the doctor came in with the sad news that the other leg would have to be amputated also.

The flyer naturally was upset, but requested that the doctor please have one of the Russian flyers drop it over England with a Hip, Hip.

The doctor agreed, and it was done.

A month later the doctor came in again and told the flyer he was sorry but to save his life he would have to amputate his right hand.

The patriotic English flyer started to make his usual request, but the doctor interrupted him and said, "I'm very sorry but I can't grant your request this time."

The pilot asked, "Why not?"

The doctor replied, "They think you're trying to escape!"

A man goes to the shrink and tells him that no one talks to him.

The doctor says, "Next."

Two friends meet on the street. One tells the other one, "Did you know Sam died?"

"Is that right. Did he leave anything?"

"Yeah, everything!"